IN THE SEWERS
OF LVOV

BLOOMSBURY READER

Discover books by Robert Marshall published by
Bloomsbury Reader at
www.bloomsbury.com/RobertMarshall

All the King's Men
In the Sewers of Lvov

IN THE SEWERS OF LVOV

The Last Sanctuary from the Holocaust

ROBERT MARSHALL

BLOOMSBURY READER

LONDON · NEW DELHI · NEW YORK · SYDNEY

This edition published in 2013 by Bloomsbury Reader

Bloomsbury Reader is a division of Bloomsbury Publishing Plc,

50 Bedford Square, London WC1B 3DP

First published in Great Britain 1990 by William Collins Sons & Co.

ISBN: 978 1 4482 1354 2
eISBN: 978 1 4482 1002 2

Visit www.bloomsburyreader.com to find out more about our authors and their books
You will find extracts, author interviews, author events and you can sign up for
newsletters to be the first to hear about our latest releases and special offers

Dedicated to the memory of Leopold Socha

Contents

Acknowledgements

This book was made possible by the selfless co-operation of four people. Dr Kristine Keren has been a tireless support throughout my research. Her constant encouragement and frankness made my task far easier than it might otherwise have been.

Dr Keren's mother, Paulina Chyrowska (Chiger) has been equally generous. Her extraordinary powers of recollection were an invaluable asset. I can never properly express my gratitude for the way she worked with me, going over the most minute details again and again. I know Mrs Chyrowska found the work exhausting, it must also have been distressing – yet she was always ready to go on.

Mundek Margulies's boundless enthusiasm seemed at times almost an act of defiance. His greatest fear was that people might not believe what had happened. Margulies is one of the bravest men I have ever met. His courage was a great source of inspiration.

Throughout Klara Margulies has been the most touching witness. Her disarming modesty, generosity and loyalty to others gave me invaluable insight. Her contribution to this book is incalculable.

I am also greatly indebted to Dr Henri Berestycki, his sister Susan Etam Berestycki and their mother Mrs Gutche Berestycki who have generously helped describe the role played by their father, Jacob. I am equally grateful to Mrs Iona Mislab for her accounts concerning her father and mother, Chaskiel Orenbach and Genia Weinberg. I would also like to thank David Lee Preston, son of Halina Wind, for his encouragement.

To the following friends and colleagues, my thanks for their kind help. David Spector whose enthusiasm for this story was its very genesis, Dr Martin Gilbert for his generous encouragement, Dr Bullen at the Imperial War Museum, Michael Fishwick and Richard Wheaton at Collins for their patience and thoroughness, Roy Davies at Timewatch for his sound advice, the staff of the Map Room at the Royal Geographical Society, Anita Lowenstein for invaluable help as a translator, along with my colleagues Jonathan Dent and Chris Mohr.

Finally, my special thanks to Clive and Bonnie Overlander for their support at a moment of crisis. No words can express ...

Robert Marshall
London, February 1990

LVOV

RIVER PELTWA

JANOWSKA ROAD

KEY:

1 GHETTO AREA
2 BARRACKS
3 PELTEWNA STREET
4 WYSOKI ZAMEK
5 PRISON
6 OPERA HOUSE
7 CHURCH OF OUR LADY OF THE
   SNOWS
8 TOWN HALL
9 SERBSKA STREET
10 STORM BASIN
11 BERNARDINSKI MONASTERY
12 MAIN RAILWAY STATION
13 JANOWSKA CONCENTRATION CAMP
14 PIATSKI (THE SANDS)

Introduction

Some time during the early 1970s an elderly Polish Jew, Jacob Berestycki was his name, wrote to his friend Ignacy Chiger about their experiences together during the war.

'Chiger,' he wrote, 'you were the one with the pen in his hand. Write it all down.'

The two men had met towards the end of 1942, in the Jewish ghetto of what was then the Polish city of Lvov. They later became members of a small group who survived the Holocaust in some of the most desperate conditions imaginable. In the thirty years since their liberation, no one had spoken in detail about what had happened and a number of people had begun to wonder whether their story would ever be told.

Only Berestycki and Chiger knew the whole story from beginning to end, and they felt that if one of them didn't set it down it might be lost. For thirty years Chiger had made notes about what had happened, but had resisted attempting a complete account. He had struggled with a conflict familiar to many survivors of the great Jewish tragedy; trying to satisfy the need to describe what had happened, while at the same time not wanting to disturb memories that had been laid to rest. According to his daughter

Kristine, Chiger's path through this conflict had been slow and painful, made more difficult by other responsibilities.

In the midst of their ordeal, Chiger had become the leader of their group and as such he felt that his account should speak for all. They had lived together under the most appalling conditions, been forced to share the most intimate aspects of their lives and in the months together witnessed both the worst and the very best of each other. Would history be served by describing everything?

By 1975 Chiger had conquered his doubts. His daughter presented him with a Polish typewriter and he began. With typical thoroughness he began with the events, as he recalled them, of 1 September 1939 and concluded with the days immediately following their liberation. It is an account of one of the most remarkable episodes of survival from the Jewish Holocaust. Six months after his work was finished Ignacy Chiger died.

In 1988, while making a documentary about this episode for the BBC series Timewatch, I met Chiger's daughter Kristine Keren and his widow Paulina. Along with Mundek and Klara Margulies, they are the last surviving members of Chiger's group able to bear witness. (A fifth survivor, Genia Weinberg, has for some years now been too unwell to recall any of what happened.) Some months after our work was finished, Mrs Keren told me about her father's manuscript and asked if I would write a book based upon it. When I saw the Chiger manuscript I realized that it was not a complete account, but a record of Chiger's own personal recollection. In that respect, it appears to be an accurate record, for, like memory itself, it reveals a great deal of detail in some parts, while elsewhere it conflates separate incidents and abbreviates others. However, it has one invaluable quality: it is extremely subjective. It was written in isolation, without reference to any of the other survivors' recollections. Nor, so far as I can tell, has it influenced the recollections of those who have survived Chiger. Even after fifteen years, his widow Paulina Chiger has still not read the manuscript.

That element of isolation prevailed amongst all the survivors. Though they have always remained close to one another, they never discussed their common wartime experiences. The subject never seemed to arise. Consequently, their private recollections, like Chiger's, remained uncontaminated. So, with five separate, highly subjective surviving versions, I set about trying to see if it would be possible to produce an account that would be faithful to all.

I have also interviewed a number of secondary sources, that is to say, the children of those members of the group who are not alive today. Their accounts are really inheritances, passed down from their parents, though cherished and indeed nourished nevertheless. As I gathered more material I expected to encounter contradictions. In the event, I was surprised at how many of the accounts tended to compliment each other, sometimes allowing me five separate perspectives of the same incident. (There were only a few contradictions and in each case I have presented the reader with all versions.) So the following is almost entirely based upon personal account. It has been built up from countless hours of interviews and recorded conversations, during which we often returned to the same incident five or six times.

Throughout all the interviews I made with the survivors I was conscious of the manner in which they were delivered. Told without inhibition, and often containing long passages of dialogue – conversations, discussions, arguments – acted out like a dramatic saga. I have drawn heavily upon this dialogue; it may not always have been what was actually said, but it is precisely how it was remembered.

Chapter I

If you stand upon the hill that rises above the city of Lvov and watch as the evening sun sets on the roofs, you might easily believe for a moment that you were somewhere else. You find spread before you an Italianate jumble of terracotta roofs, interrupted by the occasional thicket of trees or the bald dome of a church. Rising from the layers of mist the towers and spires etched in the evening light proclaim the city's heart to be in western Europe. It might be Florence.

Down below, there are districts of narrow cobbled lanes that curve and twist round the footings of medieval churches. Buildings lean out from their foundations, frowning over the pavements and the incessant clatter of pedestrians on the cobbles. Suddenly these precious little windings turn and spill into wide cosmopolitan boulevards. A walk down the Teodor Platz, or through the municipal gardens towards the opera house, evokes images of Paris or Berlin. The red and white trams jangling down the streets conjure an image of Vienna. The town hall, a stark piece of nineteenth-century utilitarianism, stands in the centre of a large piazza, embraced by a girdle of market traders and statues of classical Rome.

Given its physical bearing, a curious mixture of the Mediterranean and Germanic, of the romantic and the classical, Lvov is something of an anomaly today, standing as it does on the western fringes of the Soviet empire. For most of its history it was a Polish city, nestled in an area largely populated by Ukrainian peasants. It was a city of Poles, Jews and Ukrainians, the eastern outpost of the Austro-Hungarian empire, and had been for hundreds of years a centre of western culture and commerce on the edge of the Russian Steppes. In those days, its official name was Lemberg; only the Ukrainians called it Lvov. Today, the Poles are an aging minority, the Jews have all but disappeared and the city is dominated by Russians and Ukrainians.

By the evening, when the narrow streets have been cooled in long shadows, the market traders have folded up their stalls, swept their rubbish and gone, the sound of running water can be heard, cleansing the streets of debris. In the empty piazza, when the tram cars are silent, again the sound of water trickling from the fountains at either end; Diana amidst the flowers, Neptune with his trident. The sounds seem to drift up towards the hill that rises behind the square and eventually towers over the city.

Standing upon that hill, called Wysoki Zamek – which means High Castle – and gazing across the city you will see in the distance, rising in the hills that bound the southern limits, the river Peltwa. It flows down into the shallow valley where the city lies, and another illusion is conjured. With the river flowing into its mist, the city appears to lie at the mouth of a great harbour. Look west, into the haze and you can almost sense the presence of the sea. But there is no sea, and the river having entered the fringes of the city, suddenly disappears, becomes hidden.

From the summit of Wysoki Zamek you can see the street lights begin to wink in the evening haze, you can almost feel the heart of the city resting. The sounds will soften to the gentle wind disturbing the trees while perhaps the last of the tram cars will clatter up the boulevards. And you can hear, way off in the distance, the whistle of trains echoing long into the night.

It was March 1943.

At regular intervals, day and night, long distance trains arrived from the west loaded with soldiers from all across the Balkans, Italy, Czechoslovakia, Austria and of course Germany. They then left to make the journey east to Kiev and further. There were other trains calling at Lvov carrying a different cargo. Long processions of solidly built cattle trucks, with but a single window high up and shrouded in barbed wire. Each carried some eighty or so passengers, men, women and children, crushed together in the stench of excrement. Their destination was a place some seventy-five kilometres north of Lvov, called Belzec. These particular transports brought people from as far away as the Netherlands, France, Belgium, even Norway.

After pulling out of the main station, sometimes called the Vienna Station, on the western side of the city, the trains would head north through the marshalling yards, then enter a shallow cutting and pass beneath the Janowska Road. Despite being below street level, no one on the train could miss the massive walled compound that stood off to the right. By evening, the compound was already lit up by a web of floodlights standing all around the perimeter.

Some of the transports would stop in the marshalling yards and disgorge passengers. Carrying what possessions they had, they would be led into the compound, to the floodlit assembly ground in the centre. They believed they had come to work, but an hour or so later they were marched back to the cattle trucks

3

– naked. The scene was watched from a distance by the compound residents, who, once the travellers had departed, would emerge from their huts to begin sorting out the piles of belongings left in the centre of the assembly ground.

Once past the Janowska camp, the train would begin to arc round to the south-east, as though returning to the centre of town. At the same time, it would emerge from the cutting and climb high above the streets, along the brow of a steep embankment. Running out of the industrial fringe back into the city, the trains would rattle the first-floor windows of the apartments and offices that border the desirable part of town.

On the left-hand side of the tracks, down at the foot of the embankment, lay a neighbourhood of simple workers' cottages and tenement blocks. Nothing stirred along the little streets, no lights blazed, no evening strollers took the air. The trains hammered their way over the bridge on Peltewna Street and filled the narrow canyons of houses with thunder.

The inhabitants of the ghetto, all of them Jews, had long grown accustomed to the transports passing overhead, day and night. Those filled with soldiers would be headed east, to Tarnopol, to Kiev, to the war. During the winter, these trains became known as 'frozen meat'. If, however, the train pulled the familiar bleak cattle trucks, they were simply known as the 'Jewish Trains'.

Most people in the ghetto knew the destination of those trains from stories they had heard from the 'jumpers'. These were the terrified creatures who had squeezed out from a cattle truck and jumped, stark naked, from the train. Those who survived the fall, or the shots from guards on the train, or being captured and delivered up to their guards, those who had survived all that – and some did – made their way to the ghetto where they sought sanctuary. Their descriptions of what was happening had forewarned those who had wanted to listen.

Cutting through the northern suburbs of the city, the trains would eventually emerge into the countryside to the east, then branch off to the north – for Belzec, a journey of less than two hours. They said the ground all along the line to Belzec was littered with the bleached remains of unsuccessful 'jumpers'.[1]

* * *

The temperature had already dropped on that particular evening in March. On a single blast of a whistle, down on Peltewna Street groups of women appeared at doorways and began to file towards the centre of the street, while down towards the railway bridge, a small orchestra would begin a rousing march. The bright strains of clarinets and cymbals echoed discordantly. The orchestra had been an 'improvement' introduced by one of the ghetto's previous commandants, SS Obersturmführer Heinrich.

The last stragglers stumbled out of the buildings and drifted down towards the orchestra, watched by armed soldiers standing at intervals along the road. The women, slightly stooped with malnutrition and clutching their loose-fitting clothes about them, shuffled into a 'brigade', a squad of about fifty, while a young man in a nondescript peaked cap, one of the Jewish police, a capo, paced up and down shepherding them into place. The same scene took place every day, morning and evening, there in the shadow of the railway bridge.

Beneath the bridge, the street was barred by a pair of large wooden gates, crowned with barbed wire. Stretching from the gates, along the line of the railway in either direction, was a wood and barbed-wire fence some ten feet high. It ran up to the bridge over Zamarstynowska Street, followed that street north to

Graniczna Street where it turned left and re-crossed Peltewna Street and continued in a lazy arc back towards the railway line. By March 1943, there were 9000 souls living behind the fence.

Once the brigade had been counted, the women shuffled forwards, past the little orchestra, through the opened gates and out into the street. In her account of that day, Paulina Chiger recalled that she had not seen her husband before she was summoned to the brigade. But before leaving she had spoken with her seven-year-old daughter Kristina, leaving strict instructions where she and her younger brother were to hide if there was trouble. It had been rehearsed many times; at the first sound of footsteps, Kristina would grab young Pawel, who was only four years old, and push him into a suitcase which she then slid under the bed. Then she would dash to the corner where her mother's dressing gown hung from a nail, and hide behind it. As she waited, Kristina counted the seconds until she could get to Pawel before he suffocated.

The women walked down the centre of the road, their escorts marching along the pavements on either side. As this wretched column moved along they were jeered at by groups of men, or laughed at by children playing in the street. They marched on, heads bowed, clutching their coats tightly round their shoulders. It was not uncommon for an emboldened passer-by to leap at some unfortunate in the column and snatch their coat or jacket. It was not a criminal offence to steal from a Jew.

They marched through the heart of the city to the Schwartz und Comp., a garment factory on Uichala Street. There were a great many enterprises that had flourished on the labour of these people. Leder, Pelz-Galenterie Le-Pel-Ga, Hazet (a confectioner), Rucker (meat canning), Staedtische Werkataetten (municipal utility shops), Reinigung (refuse collection and disposal), Ostbahn (railway workshops) and others. At Schwartz und Comp. they produced military uniforms. In the summer, thousands of light green shirts, jackets and trousers; in the winter the uniforms were white. More than 3000 people, mostly women, laboured in two twelve-hour shifts to fulfil their quotas. They worked over peddle machines or conveyor belts under the eyes of managers who maintained efficiency and discipline with a rubber club.

The factory was kept running twenty-four hours a day, and a worker who failed to meet the quota was kept there fourteen, sixteen hours until it was completed. Despite the regime at Schwartz, it was one of the better places to work and there was always a queue outside to fill any vacancies. The alternative to employment was certain deportation.

A young girl of seventeen, Klara Keler, found herself assigned to the Schwartz workforce. Her father and brother had been taken many months before and had died in the Janowska camp. A little later, Klara had witnessed her mother's execution – shot dead before her eyes. So Klara and her younger sister Manya were left to fend for themselves. Almost immediately, they were separated and Klara was taken to the Janowska camp. In her account, Klara remembers having to stand in the centre of the parade ground with hundreds of other women, while an officer marched amongst their ranks ordering each to step either to the left or to the right.

Like countless others who had stood on that piece of ground, Klara had no idea of the significance of these orders. Except that on that occasion, there was someone close by who under-stood what was happening – who knew the rules. As Klara watched the officer moving slowly down the line towards her, she felt a stiff kick in the back of the leg. Then, she recalled, a woman whispered to her from behind.:

'Tell them you can sew,' she was told.

Klara looked over her shoulder at the woman behind her.

'Tell them you can sew.'

'But I don't know the first thing …'

'Just tell them you can sew!'

Klara did as she was told and the guard lent into her.

'Do you have your own machine?'

'We both have machines.' The words had come from the young woman behind her and Klara nodded in agreement.

'Yes, I have a machine.'

'To the right.'

The two of them were taken back to the ghetto. Her new companion was a woman called Esther. When Klara and Manya were reunited they moved in with Esther and her family, who lived in a block of workers' dwellings they called the 'barracks' near the gates to the ghetto. Though her new neighbours seemed a pretty rough-looking crowd, the two girls knew they were safe.

A sewing machine was found for Klara, which had to be donated to Schwartz und Comp. in return for employment. Manya never managed to get a work permit and so had to remain hidden in the barracks where some of the men always seemed prepared to hide people from the authorities.

In the same brigade was another young woman, stumbling to keep her place. She was called Halina. It wasn't her real name. She had been born Fayga Wind, but became Halina Naskiewicz, a good Catholic Pole, in an attempt to save herself. For a while it had worked, and as a good Catholic she had kept out of harm's way, peering from her room in Lvov at these pitiful women shuffling through the streets to work. The sight used to break her heart: 'it was excruciating, watching them being led with whips and dogs.'

It wasn't long, however, before Halina's deception was discovered and she was forced to join these same women. Confused, bewildered and afraid, she hid her face from the mocking eyes. She had adopted the name Halina, discarded Naskiewicz and now called herself Halina Wind.[2]

Before the new shift began, the women were addressed by an SS officer from the Janowska camp. The message he had brought was that this would be the last night shift. Other work would be found for them, but that would be the last time they had to make the journey to Schwartz und Comp. during the evening. The news was of little interest.

'Do they no longer need so many uniforms? What kind of work do they have in store? What else is there to do in this place but make uniforms?'

They laboured before their peddle machines, counting the hours till the meal break at midnight, a bowl of hot soup and some bread. In the long stretch through the night, they glanced up now and again to the frosted windows for a sign that the shift was over. Then, as the grey light of dawn appeared, the same cavalcade of exhausted women returned to the gates of the ghetto. In fact, it was not really a ghetto. Since January it had lost any vestige of being a neighbourhood for free citizens when it was declared a Juden Lager, or Julag. In March, a new notice had been erected at the entrance.

JU-LAG
RW
Lemberg

It translated: Jewish Camp, 'R' for *ruestung*, meaning munitions, and 'W' for *wirtschaft*, meaning economic production. It had effectively been transformed into a concentration camp, a place where the inhabitants slept when they were not at their labours. The people who lived there had to have employment in an approved enterprise and were assigned to specific accommodation blocks depending on where they worked. If you were without work, you were dead.

The ghetto commander was SS Obersturmführer Grzymek, a German national from the Sudetenland. His predecessor, Heinrich, had lasted but a few months before contracting spotted typhus. Grzymek's arrival had utterly transformed their lives because of his insane obsession with cleanliness. He insisted upon the highest standards of hygiene for everyone. Throughout the Julag he had erected posters proclaiming:

CLEANLINESS AND ORDER!
ORDER AND CLEANLINESS MUST BE MAINTAINED!
ORDER ABOVE ALL!

He patrolled the streets himself, entering the buildings to inspect each home while the inhabitants were at work. A smear of grease on a pane of glass, scraps of food, a heap of ashes in the stove would be cause for retribution. Grzymek was homicidal. For a tuft of stubble left unshaved he would shoot you himself; for an untidy room he would deport all the inhabitants; for the first hint of disease he would execute everyone in the building and raze the pitiful shell to the ground. His lunatic behaviour sent the population into frenzied devotions of washing, sweeping, polishing whatever they were forced to call home.

That morning, as the women returned from the last night shift, they shuffled through the gates much earlier than usual. Klara recalled, 'It was five o'clock and something was happening.' Their escorts gathered into a group like a collapsing concertina and stared ahead of them. Something was definitely happening. Gradually the women saw too. Up the street, soldiers were cursing and barking orders above the sound of children's cries. They were taking the children.

Commandant Grzymek, with a detachment of the SS and swarms of Ukrainian militia, was rounding up the children of the ghetto.

Everyone froze for a moment as they slowly took this in. A number of large flat-bed trucks was parked at the top of the road, on to which they were loading the children. Grzymek himself paced back and forth barking orders. Occasionally he would point up the street, a shot would snap through the noise and someone would fall. Meanwhile the soldiers herded small groups towards the trucks. Klara's account recorded the brutality: 'Some were dead, some were shot. But the way they just picked them up and threw them – like you would throw a piece of meat.'

Klara saw the wounded and dead simply dragged by their feet through the street. The women watched in horror as their children were taken by an arm or a leg and swung off the ground on to the back of the truck.

Finally some of the mothers made a desperate dash towards the trucks, screaming the names they had given their young ones. Some climbed on to the trucks, some were halted and then thrown on to the truck with their children. Grzymek was in complete control. There would be no chaos – though the screams and the sounds of weeping seemed to rend the heavens. Klara stood with a small group of witnesses, terrified by what played out before them. She glanced at the soldiers that were standing beside them. 'Even the guards who had come back to the ghetto with us were silenced. They just stood still,' Klara recalled.

At the top of the street, the hysteria continued unabated. In their panic to find their loved ones, most of the mothers avoided the trucks in case they found what they were looking for. Instead they ran straight into their homes, to the safe places where they had left their children the night before. They burst through doorways, opened cupboards, looked under beds, while an endless chorus of children's names rang down the alleys, up the stairwells and across the roofs. The bed clothes were still warm, the chairs had been tipped over. The children were gone.

Paulina Chiger came into her apartment and found it empty. Her cries joined with the others as she looked again and again in the wardrobe and the suitcases under the bed. She returned to the corridor and went down the stairs, to the workshop in the basement. Ignacy, her husband, was the foreman there, supervising the mending of furniture and anything else in the ghetto that needed repair.

'Where are my children?' Paulina asked.

The terror was there too, on the workmen's faces. There was no sense in trying to be calm.

'Ignacy? The children!';

'There, in the bunker.'

One of the men stepped forward. 'In the bunker. Here.'

At that moment her husband appeared, took hold of his wife and led her roughly towards the corner. He had constructed another of his ingenious hiding places behind a false wall. It was no more than a foot wide and simply made that part of the cellar seem smaller. There was a disguised entrance to one side which Ignacy removed and pushed his wife through. Breathless, she groped in the dark until she felt the familiar shapes of her children. Their hands reached for her but they didn't utter a sound. Paulina stifled her panting and in the brief pockets of silence, could hear the breathing of others.

No one knew if they were safe. There were sounds of heavy boots on the stairs and then voices ordering everyone to move.

'*Wo sind die Kinder!*'

The sounds of mumbled replies, then their hearts sank.

'*Hier ist eine nasse Wand. Das heisst, das ist frisch!*'

The plaster was still fresh, the false wall had been discovered. Further commands. One of the workers was ordered to wield the pick-axe. It came crashing through the damp wall bringing it down piece by piece. Pawel burst into tears and Paulina, taking this as her cue, cried out for them to stop. She crawled out of the hiding place with the youngest in her arms and clutching Kristina's hand. Beside her was an elderly woman who occasionally did cleaning work in the apartments and two of the carpenters.

'*Juden 'raus! 'Raus!*'

From above their heads came flashing a wide leather belt across their backs and again around their legs. As they stepped into the middle of the room, Paulina recalled thinking to herself, 'I have potassium cyanide in my hand. Three phials, for myself and the two children. I won't give it to them now. Maybe something will happen, maybe we'll be saved. If not, I've got time to put the cyanide in their mouths when we're on the truck.'

Then down the stairs another set of footsteps. It was Chiger, her husband. He turned to the officer and spoke to him in German.

'Listen, she's on the day shift now. Yesterday, they changed her from the night shift to the day shift. She's day shift now.'

Paulina clutched the cyanide tightly in her hand.

'Why did you hide them?'

'I was frightened for the children.'

The officer looked at them all, then ordered two of his men to stay while he continued his search. Above their heads they heard

13

the noises of further searches.

'You will go with the children,' said one of the soldiers to Paulina. Chiger fell to his knees.

'No, no!'

He begged with such humility, Paulina recalled. 'He removed his watch and offered it to them. They took it but were not moved. As his pleas became more desperate, they seemed more incensed and one of the soldiers brought the butt of his rifle down on my husband's head.'

Blood began to run from a deep cut above his eye. It was hopeless. There was no reason to hope any more, life was simply whatever these men had in store for them. But moments later, miraculously, the terms were changed.

'All right. One of the children will stay with you, the other goes with her. You choose.'

Chiger and Paulina glanced at each other while this new situation sank in. 'It only made my husband more desperate and his pleas became even more dramatic.' He begged them as though he were so much dust on the floor. He lowered himself to the ground, he cried up to these two giants.

'Let them stay. Let them stay! How can I choose between one child and another?' He took from his pocket a picture of the children and held it before him like a talisman, as if it might ward off the tragedy.

Meanwhile, Paulina had been carefully watching the soldiers and saw some small opportunity for a respite. She noticed they were mildly curious about two bags that had been slung over her shoulder when she emerged from the bunker. Paulina slowly lowered them to the ground and showed the soldiers the food that was packed inside. 'It was put in the bunker with the children. We didn't know how long we might have to be in there,' Paulina recalled.

The food, such an unlikely gambit, seemed to ease the situation. Taking from the bag some biscuits, a handful of bread and sardines she passed these tributes to the Germans, who devoured them. These men had been hungry. They took the bags and emptied the contents on the floor. There was medicines for the children and perhaps some clothes. Eventually one of them declared through a mouthful of food that they could all stay. At that moment, a squad of Ukrainian militia burst into the work room and ordered Paulina and the children up to the street. The Germans resented this disregard for their authority and one of them spat out,

'*Nein. Diese Kinder bleiben hier!*'

The Ukrainians, confused but unquestioning, departed. A few minutes later another squad arrived, equally determined to follow Grzymek's orders. Again the soldiers denied them permission. Paulina seized the moment to improve the situation.

'Can we all return to our apartment? And would one of you accompany us up the stairs. There are Ukrainians on every landing?'

Throughout all this, her fist stayed tightly closed around the three phials of cyanide. Once back inside their rooms, Paulina spoke calmly to the solider.

'Would you like something else to eat?'

'Scrambled eggs.'

'How many eggs?'

'Six.'

As this curious domestic scene unfolded, they were joined by Chiger's brother-in-law, Kuba Leinwand. Kuba, a tall distinguished-looking man, worked at a large paint factory. Before the war he had been a manager at the plant. The Germans had welcomed his expertise and kept him on there, though with far less responsibility.

The children had settled in a corner, Chiger had staunched

15

the bleeding and was nursing his wound while Paulina made conversation with the German. She spoke with a natural air of self-confidence. Her family had been wealthy, enjoyed a considerable degree of social importance and, consequently, Paulina had not been brought up to avert her eyes from anyone's gaze.

The soldier noticed a bar of soap on the sink. Paulina reached across and handed it to him. In the midst of all this, sounds of terror carried up from the street. Over the sound of persistent wailing, Grzymek's voice could be heard barking orders to his men. Kristina went to the window and peered down. She saw in the courtyard below rows of women, seated on the ground – waiting. When the transport arrived they were loaded aboard and taken away. Paulina turned Kristina from the window and told her to go back to the other end of the room. Meanwhile, the German finished his eggs and announced that he was going offduty. Paulina wondered how much goodwill she had purchased.

'Before you go, my cousin is downstairs. She's in trouble. Maybe you can help her.' But his eyes were upon the gold watch on Paulina's wrist.

'Do you want my watch? I'll give it to you. My cousin, downstairs. Her parents are at the factory now, on the day shift. Like me, she had been on the night shift and was changed to the day. Perhaps you can explain this to them.'

He left with the watch and her cousin's name. Paulina watched from the window as the German spoke with one of his colleagues in the street. He in turn called over one of the Jewish police, the men in the nondescript peaked caps, and gave him an order. Some moments later, the policeman emerged from the entrance of the building with Paulina's cousin and led her to the transports.

The day grew older and the *Aktion* continued throughout. By sunset 1000, perhaps 2000 people had been transported – dead or alive. Eventually the wailing ceased and a sullen quiet descended on the houses. It became quite still again, as though everyone had been drained of emotion. People sat in silence, trying to absorb what had happened, as grief and shock settled slowly into their consciousness. Suddenly Kristina heard a stifled cry and the sound of something hitting the pavement outside. She leapt to her feet. Paulina glanced out of the window and managed to stop her daughter before she could see.

'Don't look, Krisia. Don't go to the window.'

On the roof of their building, a small group of women had gathered. With their children gone they had lost their motherhood. In the depth of their grief, they had sought out each other's company, and one by one jumped into the space before them.

Chapter II

After what became known as the March Action, the most valuable commodity in the Julag was poison. The Lvov pharmacies reported massive purchases of prussic acid and cyanide, which made its way to the other side of the railway line through the black-market. It was a trade the German authorities did nothing to curtail. If they could induce the Jews themselves to expedite Nazi policies through terrorizing them, then there would be obvious savings in manpower and resources.

As usually happened after an *Aktion*, the community did what it could to heal itself while trying to pick up the shreds of their lives. At the start of the occupation they might have been numbed with shock or grief, but after nearly two years most of the population had become hardened to these barbarities. Fear and grief remained companions. The injured hid themselves from view while the rest gave thanks for their good fortune.

Chiger's wound had been more serious than at first suspected. His eye had closed up and when, after a few days, he was able to open it, he could see nothing with it. But his wife and children were still alive and what was that compared to an eye? He was still able to move about and work, there was everything to be grateful for.

Chiger was responsible for running a small workshop and team of workers to maintain the fabric of the Julag. His men roamed the streets of the Julag repairing furniture, windows, plumbing; keeping everything up to the standard expected by Grzymek. One of the men who worked under Chiger was a dwarfish individual who made up for his lack of stature by the size of his heart: Jacob Berestycki was a locksmith from the town of Lodz; quietly spoken and a devout Chasid.[3] Klara recalled seeing him often, 'sitting under the tree outside the barrack, heating his tea over a small fire'.

Though Chiger hardly knew him, Berestycki was somewhat in awe of his boss. Being a stranger to Lvov, he knew little about Chiger except that he was clearly a man of some importance within the community, and not only because he had some say over the lives of people who worked under him. He was held in far greater esteem than that of a mere maintenance foreman.

Ignacy Chiger's influence was inherited from his father, Jacob Chiger, who before the war had been one of the leaders of the Jewish Workers' Community. Under the occupation, Jacob Chiger represented the workers on the Judenrat, the Jewish council made up of lawyers, doctors and other notables of the community, which was established by the Germans to ensure the fullest co-operation in the running of their Jewish policies. As the size of the ghetto was reduced and so became more crowded, Chiger's father had done what he could to ease the conditions. He tried to ensure everyone had work, food and some kind of suitable bathing and toilet facilities. It was said that his efforts earned him the respect, even love, of not just the unskilled workers, but eventually the entire community. But on 23 January 1943, the Judenrat was abolished and Chiger's father and mother were executed. The workers in the Julag had immediately turned to their patron's son 'and begged him to take care of them, like his father had done'. Chiger had precious little authority, but what he had he used to the limit.

About the only thing Berestycki did know about Chiger was his reputation for building hiding places, or 'bunkers'. He had built them everywhere and for anyone who asked. Being responsible for maintenance, Chiger would discover work that had to be done in his client's room, and under the guise of repairing a pipe or patching up some cracks, he would secretly construct a concealed hiding place.

It was something he had assumed was a secret from his workmates, yet Berestycki had noted these operations with quiet interest. He rarely spoke to Chiger and was hardly spoken to. The two of them were as distant as manager and labourer, yet they had one thing in common: the conviction that their days were numbered, that the Julag itself was living on borrowed time.

Chiger had been certain of this from the day Grzymek had arrived. On the first morning he was seen inside the ghetto walls, he had set his mark upon their lives. There had been an inspection before the brigades marched off to work and in a calculated act of brutality, Grzymek had suddenly attacked one of the Ukrainian militiamen. Claiming that the man was slovenly dressed, he had personally meted out twenty-five blows with his whip. Afterwards, Grzymek had marched up and down the ranks of workers, while the steady crunch of his boots and the swish of his long leather coat were the only sounds to be heard. The effect upon everyone was stunning. In his remarkable book *The Death Brigade*, Leon Wells wrote that Grzymek's previous posting had been to the Polish town of Rawa Ruska, where, it was rumoured, not one single Jew had survived. He had become known as a 'ghetto liquidator'.

On the surface, life within the Julag continued as before. Each morning the brigades assembled and departed to the bright tunes of the orchestra. Then, in the evening, they returned exhausted, shuffling off to their rooms and the comfort of sleep. In reality, however, the Julag was alive with desperate activity. During the day, while the workers were away, Grzymek patrolled with a squad of soldiers spreading terror up and down the streets with impressive thoroughness. They moved quietly down corridors in search of children that had escaped the earlier *Aktion*. If they sighted a child through a window, or hidden in some cavity, the marksmen would silently lay the quarry at the end of his bead and shoot. As though clearing rabbits from a country estate, Grzymek moved through his domain.

Meanwhile, ordinary men and women had stirred themselves into a frenzy to discover some means of escape. Rooms buzzed with conspiracies, friends spoke in guarded whispers and suspicion flourished. Chiger had resolved that his only priority would be Paulina and his children. With Kuba's help he constructed new bunkers: a secret cavity beneath the window in the bathroom and another in a similar place in the kitchen. Always the same technique of creating a false wall to widen the window sill or to make the bay more shallow. No matter that the last one had been discovered, it was essential to provide some kind of sanctuary for the children while he, Kuba and his wife were away at work.

Day after day, Grzymek's footsteps echoed up and down the corridors. Kristina and Pawel clutched each other in their narrow space, trying to control the urge to cry out. She recalled:

'I will never forget the fear I had, being alone there with my little brother. Sometimes we were on our own all day. We

21

didn't cry. We weren't allowed to cry and when we heard something, we hardly even breathed. The fear was unimaginable …'

In fact the Julag had become riddled with hiding places. Not, by any means, all Chiger's work. It seemed as though everyone had constructed disguised bunkers and false cavities in the backs of cupboards, under floor-boards or in ceilings. One of the most ingenious had been built in a cellar beneath a kitchen, where a false wall had been constructed providing a space of some three metres by ten, but with no access to it from the cellar. The entrance was through a hole in the ceiling, that is, through the floor of the kitchen above. In fact, through a cast-iron stove. To get into the bunker, the iron top of the stove, the grates and ashes, had to be lifted and slid to one side. Then the fugitives lowered themselves through the body of the stove, through the floor and down a rope into the cavity below. The last one down slid the cast iron top and grates back into place.

As if Grzymek's patrols weren't enough for the Chigers, a few weeks after the March Action, Untersturmführer Gebauer paid a visit to Schwartz und Comp. He was the second-in-command at the Janowska camp and his visit meant only one thing, he needed more labourers. The women were assembled outside, while he marched between them directing them to the left or the right. There had been rumours that the factory would soon be closed down and now Gebauer's presence seemed to confirm it.

At the end of the counting, Paulina found herself chosen for the camp, and was marched with about 500 women down the Janowska Road. At the end of the day, Chiger was given the news and with it, small comfort. The women had not been transported permanently, but would return to the Julag at the end of each day and be marched back to the camp in the morning.

The regime inside the Janowska camp bore no resemblance to the Julag in town. Fritz Gebauer shared responsibility with his superior, Obersturmführer Gustav Wilhaus, for creating that regime. Apparently there was little love lost and much less co-operation between these two men, yet together they had succeeded in creating an establishment that had no rival in eastern Poland. Conditions behind the tall brick and concrete walls were so nightmarish, that the men who had created them acknowledged the hopelessness of the place with their own black humour. Just inside the gates, Gebauer had erected a scaffold from which a number of nooses were slung. Each morning, he suggested to the workers that whenever it became too much for anyone, they had his personal permission to climb the scaffold and put his or her head inside the noose. Many took this option.

Wilhaus was something of a sportsman. He rode the grounds of his establishment on horseback with a favourite Alsatian at his heels. It was not uncommon for him to be seen on the front porch of his house with a rifle, shooting at people on the parade ground as though they were ducks in a shooting gallery.

In April the tension was raised higher than usual by stirring news from Warsaw. There were rumours of a revolt in the ghetto. On 19 April 1943, underground elements in the Warsaw ghetto, armed with rifles and light machine-guns, began firing upon German guards. Having raised the Polish Flag and the Jewish Star of David on the roof of the tallest building in the ghetto, the declaration of defiance was made. Rumours and then rumours of rumours filtered down through the various partisan groups at bay in the countryside about the heroic uprising in Warsaw. Soon a band of perhaps twenty young men in the Lvov Julag began collecting weapons and ammunition and storing them in the bakery. The news had also sent a frisson of unease through the rulers of the Julag. SS General Katzmann, head of the SS throughout Galicia, sent orders for greater vigilance throughout the province and Grzymek's patrols were increased.

With the tension almost at breaking point, Chiger continued obsessively in his search for places to hide his family. One morning in April, he had assigned Berestycki to work with him in and around the barracks by the main gates. They made an odd couple, the little man cantering beside the tall, broad-shouldered Chiger. Ignacy had been something of an athlete in his youth. His large, noble head sat proudly upon a frame which, though withered with malnutrition, still retained some vestige of his active youth. Yet the spark of amiability had dimmed from his eyes. According to the Berestycki account, Chiger seemed harder, more diffident. Like many people in the Julag, Chiger had generated about himself the air of a man determined to survive. 'He was remote, difficult to talk to,' was Berestycki's impression.

Looking around themselves, Chiger and Berestycki would have seen a shell of a community. Before the war, the Jewish population of Lvov had been more than 100,000. By June 1941, that had swelled to 160,000 with refugees from the west. From the best accounts available, by the spring of 1943, that number had been cut down to just 7000 with perhaps another 4000 in the Janowska camp.

As they strode together, Berestycki summoned the courage to speak.

'You know, Chiger, it is no longer safe to build bunkers.'

'What are you talking about?'

'Don't you think you're taking a terrible risk?'

Chiger remained aloof.

24

'Look, I know you've built a number of bunkers for your family. I uncovered one of them myself. If I know where they are, so do others.'

'What of it?'

'It's not a safe thing to do. You cannot trust people like you used to. Information can be sold.'

Berestycki was not a man to threaten. He was a pious Chasid with a temperament born of simple honesty. But he was sharp. He had a talent for examining a problem and seizing upon the solution.

'I have a better plan …' he continued, '… but we have to trust each other.'

Berestycki explained to Chiger that right beneath their feet was the perfect place to hide – the sewers. Looking down Peltewna Street, they would have seen a line of manhole covers running straight towards them. These led down to the Peltwa, an underground river from which the street took its name. All the city's sewers ran into the Peltwa.

None of this would have been news to Chiger. Before the turn of the century, the Peltwa flowed through the heart of the city like an oily canal, into which ran untreated sewage. The stench during the summer was unspeakable. Then, around the turn of the century, an Italian engineering company constructed the present sewer system. In the course of which they diverted the river underground, through a massive chamber that ran the length of the city. It emerged again some distance north of the Julag perimeter and flowed out into the countryside.

It had been common during an *Aktion* to see people lifting a manhole in the street, trying to escape to the Peltwa and eventually to the open countryside. But it was a pointless exercise, for the Germans stationed guards at the opening to the river and picked off the fugitives as they emerged. Chiger knew that the Peltwa was no escape, but Berestycki was convinced the sewers might be a refuge.

'I have an idea of building a tunnel down to the Peltwa – to the sewers, where we can hide. We find some part of the sewers, make it habitable and we could hide there for weeks.'

According to Berestycki, Chiger was unimpressed with the suggestion, but the little man persisted.

'We need to build an access that can't be seen from the street. Something we can disguise after we have gone. I know just the place.'

The Berestycki account claims that the discussion continued cautiously and though Chiger was not keen on the idea, he 'allowed himself to be convinced'. This runs at some variance with Chiger's own account and rather than arbitrate between the two, I will offer the reader both. According to Chiger: 'I decided to see if one of my plans might have a chance of succeeding. The plan was for us to try to escape to the sewer. My friend Berestycki agreed that this might work and we began to discuss how we should go about it.'

In Berestycki's account, however, Chiger's co-operation had been sought because if the shaft was to be built, Berestycki needed to be excused from his work. He implied others were involved when he claimed, 'We couldn't do anything without Chiger's permission.'

Here is Chiger's account again: 'We included in our discussion a man called Weiss. We planned to dig a tunnel from his room down to the sewers where we would look for a dry shelter.'

Weiss's room in the barrack had been calculated to be directly above the line of manholes. Weiss was also Berestycki's neighbour.

According to Klara, who shared a room next door, 'Weiss was a tall, thin man with blond hair', whom she found 'quite frightening'. The barrack where they lived was one of a pair of one story terraces built at right angles to Peltewna Street. They were really simple workers' dwellings, constructed by the city authorities before the war. Inside, a long corridor ran the full length and leading off this were perhaps fifty, simple two-room apartments. Since the ghetto had been created, entire families had been forced into each room, sharing the public bathrooms with perhaps two hundred others. There was no gas, little electricity and water had to be fetched from a stand pipe outside. Cooking was done on small kerosine stoves, if they had one, amongst the mattresses and other possessions. Weiss shared the room with his mother, wife and daughter, and the young woman from Turka named Halina Wind.

Berestycki had not explained more than was necessary to Chiger, about Halina and one or two others living nearby being illegal residents. He and Weiss had made a habit of providing shelter and forged papers for any unfortunates that came their way.

'Halina had escaped from the Weisenhof prison and so Weiss and Berestycki had taken her in,' wrote Chiger, who was then introduced to Weiss and his immediate family. In his account, the project was developed exclusively between himself, Berestycki and Weiss: 'The three of us began to plan the project, knowing that Weiss's room would be a safe place from which to work.' However, it is clear from other accounts that there were many more people involved, and perhaps it says much for the secrecy that enveloped the project that Chiger knew nothing of the others. It also seems probable, at least from the Berestycki account, that he and Weiss had been discussing the idea for some time before mentioning it to Chiger. Once the maintenance supervisor had been involved, his contacts with the others were kept to a minimum. According to the Berestycki account: 'In the beginning, they were afraid of each other as well as what was outside. They had not learnt to trust each other yet.'

Over the next few days, Weiss held a number of secret meetings in his room, from which the simple idea was transformed into a complex operation. As Weiss provided the location for the shaft and therefore assumed greater risk, it was appropriate that he also assumed command of the project and responsibility for enlisting the help of others, such as two engineers, whose names are now forgotten, who also lived in the barrack. They were recruited to conduct surveys of the sewers and try and solve the obvious technical problems. They slipped down a manhole at night with a torch and sketch pad, and made crude drawings of the lay-out. They described a large vaulted chamber through which flowed the Peltwa and into which a number of smaller 'channels' emptied. It was recommended that they dig from one of these channels, up towards Weiss's room. This would have solved the problem of disposing of the soil from their diggings, but then their calculations would have had to have been absolutely precise, if they were to surface at the right spot. It would clearly be easier to dig downwards, but how to dispose of the earth? The problem was solved with the discovery of a shallow cellar beneath the barracks' floor. It was not really a cellar, more like a deep crawl-space amongst the foundations, deep enough to work in. Once under the floor, they could dig the shaft unnoticed. Chiger recalled the plan they all agreed upon. 'We decided to dig down through the floor of the cellar beneath Weiss's room and, by carefully measuring, aimed for a dried-out side channel of the Peltwa, where we could hide.'

Another recruit was a friend of Berestycki's, Mundek Margulies, a remarkably quick-witted and resourceful man. He had helped run a small barber's shop before the Germans had captured Lvov and had since found work at Textalia, a textile co-operative. He was remarkable in that he had never had the correct papers to live in the ghetto, had been marked down for deportation to the death camps long ago and yet had survived and indeed flourished. Although he marched to Textalia every morning, he did very little work there for he knew almost nothing about textiles and little more about barbering. To most people in Julag he was one of the most resourceful black-marketeers. Margulies had a reputation for being able to get hold of almost any commodity through sources on the other side of the wire. He bartered or traded textiles or leather from the co-operative; suits, coats, silver or other valuables from his fellow inmates, in return for fresh eggs, milk, cheese, razor blades – anything he could lay his hands on. If you needed it, Margulies could get it. He operated just outside the gates, usually dealing with Ukrainian farmers and traders. Weiss approached Margulies:

'We need someone we can trust. Someone with a few brains, a little orientation, understand?'

This short, robust fellow with powerful arms and a tenacious will to survive would be an essential asset if the project was to succeed. Margulies soon met some of the others who were involved: Shulim Weinberg and two brothers from the town of Radzyn named Chaskiel and Itzek Orenbach. Margulies also recalls seeing Chiger at one of Weiss's meetings, though Chiger doesn't mention this.

The first priority was to construct an entrance to the cellar in Weiss's room. To do the work properly, they needed the right tools, which is where Chiger came in. He explained: 'Since Berestycki and I worked together in the Julag, we were able to work out the plans and get hold of the necessary materials without being discovered.'

Chiger also 'covered' for Berestycki when he was at work in Weiss's room. They cut out a rectangle of floor boards and then took a stone slab, in fact a paving stone from the street, to put in their place. It gave the impression that there was nothing but solid earth beneath. A rug and a table were placed over it just in case. Once beneath Weiss's room, Chiger constructed another of his partitions, made of wood and plaster, to disguise their diggings, should anyone get into the cellar from another route. Then they began digging. Weinberg's beautiful wife Genia recalled the ingenious method of working in Weiss's room.

'When they were working on the tunnel, they placed a table over the hole in Weiss's floor and then spread a sheet over a table so it looked like a tablecloth, draped down to the floor. Down in the cellar, they worked with spoons and forks, digging at the earth, while people sat at the table and played cards, talked or ate. If the Germans came into the room – they saw nothing.'

While the work progressed, the rhythms of the Julag continued. In the evenings, Paulina returned from her work in the Janowska camp and released her children from the bunker in the kitchen. Chiger returned from his labours a little later and she would recount ever more devastating horrors being inflicted on the women in the camp.

'Gebauer doesn't like women with grey hair. If he sees one grey hair, he shoots them. He is killing women every day.'

Chiger listened to these accounts and decided that if Paulina continued to work at the camp it only increased the likelihood of her being murdered. He decided she would simply have to go missing.

'You're not going back to the camp. You'll stay here,' he told her.

Paulina thought the idea just as dangerous. 'They know I should be up at the Janowska Road. Grzymek comes round during the day looking for people like me.'

Chiger claimed he had a new place where she and the children could hide. He told her to pack some warm clothing for living underground. Paulina took out the children's cheap felt boots, but Kristina had recently been given a new pair of summer sandals.

'No. Where we are going you won't need them.'

But Kristina was adamant. The felt boots had to be packed away with everything else and they moved across to the barrack, Krisia proudly wearing her new sandals. They were led down through a hole in someone's floor, to a space where Chiger had already set up a simple bed and some benches. While he was away at the workshop and Kuba at the paint factory, Paulina and the children sat quietly beneath Weiss's room. Strangers came and went, taking their turn to work on the shaft and ignored the family that was camped beside them. Whether Weiss and the others saw their presence as an unnecessary risk, we do not know. Chiger was loath to leave them there for long and contrived to make regular visits, bringing tools he had taken from the workshops. By now, Chiger's brother-in-law had also been drafted on to the project and they both took turns down the shaft.

At first, the work was daunting. They had to break through a solid concrete floor and at times it seemed that they would never do it. They could not attack the concrete with a pick or deliver a

31

full-hearted blow on the chisel in case the noise attracted attention. So, painstakingly, they picked and chipped their way through, at first with spoons and forks, then eventually with tools from the workshop. Finally they made it through to the soft earth beneath.

Boards were brought down to shore up the sides and a cover made of another paving stone was used to disguise the entrance. They succeeded in digging an extremely narrow shaft, down to a depth of about one and a half metres – about the height of the average man. At that point their progress was abruptly halted. Beneath their feet was more solid stone. They had struck the roof of a sewer chamber.

Working in a space barely wider than a man, they chipped and scraped away at the solid limestone. They presumed they were working towards some small channel that formed part of the sewer network, but they were also aware that they might in fact be directly over the river Peltwa. Therefore, if they broke through the ceiling, might they not just fall straight into the river?

They worked on cautiously, chipping at the limestone at their feet. In fact, the stone they were trying to break up had been carefully laid into place by one of an army of masons during the 1890s. Each piece had been hewn into a shallow arc, sometimes nearly a metre long and perhaps twenty-five centimetres wide. No one could guess how thick it was. The only people who knew that had left Lvov forty years ago.

The Italian engineering company had constructed the system by damming the Peltwa while a deep tunnel was bored beneath the city. The floor of this tunnel would be more than forty feet below street level. This was then lined with stone and cement, while at the same time the roof was constructed overhead. The masons, working atop wooden scaffolding, had carved away the soil in front of them and then shouldered each massive stone into place.

It quickly became apparent to Weiss and his men that the pieces fitted together with the precision of a Roman arch. Each block had been braced against the weight of the soil above, transmitting that weight sideways through each neighbouring piece down to the floor of the chamber. Now the blocks of stone were being attacked from above – and were easily withstanding each blow. If the intruders were going to get through they would have to demolish the limestone into tiny fragments. And this is precisely what they did. Late one evening, Chiger, Berestycki and Weiss were at work, chipping away at the material until one of their blows passed straight through into space.

A moment later, the fragments clattered somewhere below, then suddenly a massive block collapsed beneath their feet and crashed with a resounding explosion on to something solid. They were through.

Chapter III

Up through the shaft came the odour of stale air which soon filled the cellar. There was also an ominous roar – an incessant rush of noise. It was the Peltwa. Chiger, Berestycki and Weiss were terribly excited by the breakthrough and decided, there and then, to go further.

No one recalls who was the first down the shaft, but the story was the same for all. They had to lower themselves feet first down to the stone layer at the bottom of the shaft. At that point they found the narrow aperture left by the limestone block. The first of the three squeezed his hips through and inched downwards, clinging to an outstretched hand from above. Feet flayed about until they made contact with something solid – a wall? Now braced against it, he searched with his boots for the solid floor they believed was there. Chiger recalled: '… the chamber caused the noise of the rushing water to be magnified. Even the smallest sound would echo through the tunnel.' Compared with the relative quiet of the cellar, the noise in the chamber seemed almost deafening. Descending into this hopelessly dark and noisy environment of the sewer, Chiger '… was seized by a great sense of being lost and enveloped by a fear that caused me actually to tremble.'

The drop from the hole in the roof of the chamber to what lay below was literally a leap into the unknown. The noise of the river was so loud, it seemed right beneath their feet. The person descending had finally to let go of the arm above him and he was on his own, slipping further and further away. At the very point when his shoulders were level with the limestone lining, with very little shaft left to purchase, his feet scraped against solid ground. One more heave downwards and he was standing securely.

Eventually all three stood together beneath the shaft. The sound of the water was now deafening. Someone stumbled to the floor, grasped a large lump of limestone that had been dislodged from the roof and hurled it out before him. It crashed into the water. With their eyes still not properly adjusted to the gloom, they slowly felt their way about until they had established that they were standing on a narrow ledge some three feet wide, beyond which, though they could not see it, was the Peltwa. Had they dipped a foot into the water they would have been shocked at the strength of the current. The water seems to pull you in even when pressed against the wall, and this is not merely an illusion. The sensation is caused by the wall which is actually a vault that arches up from the floor and across the river to the other side. Pressed against it you are forced to lean forwards, giving you the impression of being pushed towards the water.

For Chiger, those first moments in the sewer were a nightmare: 'It was so dark we couldn't even see each other, and the overwhelming sense of isolation paralysed us so that we could not force a single sound from our throats. It reminded me of Orpheus's descent into Hades. Not an imagined myth, but the real Hades.' About the only tangible fact they had absorbed was that the ledge they were on might be some form of bank – a pathway, that ran along the length of the river – but they were in

35

no mood to explore. After only a few minutes, they knew they had had enough and they were overcome by an urge to scramble out again.

Once back in the room they were overcome with a sense of almost childish delight. Chiger stood staring down into the shaft, beaming with self-satisfaction. It had terrified them, it was in no real sense a sanctuary – but it was a start. Chiger broke the news to Paulina. Despite their terror, the three men had already resolved to return. Paulina came down to the cellar with the children to watch them go. Someone had fetched a torch and its narrow beam seemed to embolden them for the return to Hades. One by one they slid themselves through the cellar floor, out of sight. From their light they could now easily see the Peltwa rushing at their feet. They could also just about see the far side, about eight metres across, with a mirror of the ledge they stood on. They flashed the torch up and down the length, but their light was too weak and it was smothered by darkness just a few meters from where they stood.

Nevertheless, it gradually became clear what a remarkable piece of work surrounded them. They were standing within a massive vaulted chamber, constructed from carved limestone blocks that formed a perfect semi-circle up and over the Peltwa. At its height it was perhaps five metres above the water. From bank to bank the river was six metres across and seemed to flow over a smooth bed of limestone which gradually declined away from the ledge to a depth of almost two metres.

Standing there in that vast vault of stone, they talked excitedly to each other about what they saw. They were in a completely new environment – somewhere where it was quite easy to forget the world above. With the torch held before him like a shield, Chiger began to lead them along the ledge. But almost immediately they were stopped short. A voice from behind cut through the roar of the river.

'What are you doing here?'

The three men were suddenly rooted to the spot, illuminated by powerful lanterns. Who ever they were – and there was more than one lantern – they addressed the three in Polish.

'I said what are you lot doing here?'

'You're all finished,' said another. 'We'll have to tell the Gestapo.'

'They've come down from the ghetto. They're finished all right,' said the first.

The captives stared blindly into the light of the lanterns. Weiss somehow gathered up his wits and spoke to them.

'We dug down from a cellar, through that shaft. We're looking for a shelter. Somewhere to hide.'

'There's nowhere to hide down here. Where do you think you are?'

Weiss continued, 'We planned to find somewhere where we could hold up, where we could stay hidden for a few weeks. Perhaps you might know somewhere? There's no need to hand us over, just tell us where we can hide.'

'You know there's no escape out of these sewers.' It was a third voice. There were three of them. He stepped forward and allowed himself to be illuminated by the lanterns.

Chiger spoke now. 'Of course, we understand that. We had not planned to escape, but to hide. That's what we meant. There must be some pipe or hole down here where we can sit, sleep, cook.'

'Cook food?' They began to laugh.

'We won't do any harm, we just want to save ourselves and our friends,' said Jacob.

'How many of you are there?' asked the illuminated one.

'Perhaps less than ten,' said Chiger.

'Ten?'

'How did you say you got down here?'

'We dug the shaft from the cellar, under my house. It's right above us.'

'Through the stone and concrete?'

'Slowly, we did it. Yes.'

'You know, we heard you. For the past day or so, we've been hearing digging in this area and so we came to investigate. We're with the sewer authority. It's our job to be down here. We do maintenance. Anyway we heard the digging so we came to investigate. We had trouble trying to locate exactly where the noises were coming from, but when we heard you breaking through you were easy to find.'

There was something oddly easy-going about this man. He spoke without menace, with a hint of good humour. The immediate threat seemed to have gone.

'I'm impressed by your ingenuity. Show me where you've come from. I want to see for myself.'

Weiss took Chiger's arm to stop him, but he was shrugged off.

'What can he do up there that he can't do from down here? We have no choice,' Chiger explained.

The sewer men also held a conference. The first two were not impressed by the jovial one's curiosity. He pointed to the hole in the chamber roof.

'This is awful. This is so unprofessional. How do you expect people to crawl through that?'

'We're not professional miners,' said Chiger. 'We don't know how to do this kind of work.'

The man laughed and then struggled up into the shaft. Chiger and the others watched him disappearing towards the cellar and could do nothing to stop him. When he had wriggled his head and shoulders clear of the cellar floor, he paused and gazed around the room – and eventually upon Paulina and her children.

It was a momentous, decisive instant shared between Paulina and the stranger. As their eyes met they each seemed to ask a question – tacitly enquiring if the other could be trusted. 'Suddenly, up popped this face – not my husband's, but a complete stranger's. I immediately took hold of Pawel and Krisia and hugged them to me.' For Paulina, the moment seemed to last forever. She hugged Krisia and Pawel, all that was most precious, and waited. Suddenly, his face exploded into a magnificent smile and the tension dissolved.

He hauled himself up into the low cellar and nodded politely to the woman with her arms around her children. He was followed by Chiger, Berestycki and Weiss. By the time the other sewer workers had arrived the little space was quite crowded. Chiger introduced his wife and explained to her the scene that had taken place down below. Paulina remained unmoved, her arms shielding her two children from this extraordinary intrusion. Who were these strangers that had emerged from the sewers?

The jovial one introduced himself as Leopold Socha. With him was, Stefak Wroblewski who smiled and shook hands. The third member, the foreman of the group, was Jerzy Kowalow. He nodded to all but said little. Polish sewer workers, maintenance engineers – they were no one important. They wore simple cloth caps, heavy work clothes and tall rubber boots, suspended by braces over their shoulders.

The six men splayed themselves across the benches and the sewer workers listened to Weiss and the others. What was to be done? Was there any way they would help? Was there somewhere in the sewers they could hide? Could they help them find it?

'I think we can help you, but we need to be paid for it,' Socha declared up front. Now they were on terms everyone understood. What sort of place did they want to hide in? When did they want to go there? What sort of preparations would be necessary? Eventually the discussion turned to the central question of payment.

'You have to understand, there are three of us who have to agree to help you. Any one of us could give you away. If we betray you we become heroes, but if we try and help and we get caught …'

'I know. You and your family will be shot.'

'Shot? They would hang my wife and children from the lampposts!'

As Socha said this, he didn't betray a hint of menace but retained the air of confident good humour which seemed so alien to Weiss and the others. Throughout their discussion, Chiger concentrated intensely on Socha's face, searching for the slightest hint of doubt or anxiety. Occasionally he saw flitting across his round, chubby face the unmistakable evidence of some inner struggle. While Socha carried the conversation back and forth – examining the pros and cons – there was a silent 'weighing of the situation inside his breast'. No one, not even Socha, was absolutely certain at that point how the scales would come down. After some time, Chiger could see no evidence that Socha's struggle had been resolved, so he decided to make the first move.

'I shall give you some money now, on account. You and your colleagues can talk about it and perhaps you might think of somewhere suitable for us down there. We can meet here tomorrow and you report what you've decided.'

'What are you doing?' Weiss leapt towards Chiger. 'You're giving them money? Are you crazy?'

Weiss was furious. Not just because they had been offered money for nothing, but Chiger's unilateral decision to take matters into his own hands usurped Weiss's authority. Weiss took Chiger and Berestycki to one side and the three of them began to argue. Weiss was convinced Chiger was about to throw away all their hard work at the very moment of their triumph. He would not allow it. Chiger saw it differently. If they were going to trust these people to help them, then purchasing a little goodwill in advance would do no harm. Besides, it was his money and if he wanted to give it to someone on account, who could stop him.

'What else can we do? Whether I give them the money or not, they can still betray us. We are in their hands.'

Chiger turned to Socha and handed him a roll of notes.

'Let's arrange a rendezvous, here, tomorrow. You can tell me then what you've decided.'

Chiger was a fair judge of character. He said afterwards that as he handed the money across to the sewer worker, he was confident that Socha would return. Paulina, who had been watching, recalled the incident: 'That was the moment that the deal was sealed. I could see it in Socha's face.'

Socha and the others got to their feet and explained that they had to get back to work. As they parted, Socha had turned to Chiger. 'Everything will turn out well.'

As soon as the sewer workers had descended through the shaft, those in the cellar were left with a deep sense of unease. They were now completely vulnerable. All their plans – their very existence – could now be obliterated by a single word from Socha and his friends. The excitement of breaking through to the chamber beneath their feet was forgotten and a familiar

41

anxiety gnawed away at their nerves. The indelible image of Socha's beaming face seemed the only guarantee for their future.

As promised, Socha returned the following day and every day after that, still beaming that air of good humour. He made himself familiar with the children, lifting them on to his lap and telling them stories. Pawel seemed to develop an immediate attachment to this cheerful new uncle and that in itself was evidence of something. Of course he would help them find somewhere, but he let them know that it wasn't going to be easy. They did no further work on the shaft for the next few days while all their plans were suspended.

Eventually Socha reported that the others had agreed to cooperate and help find somewhere that could be made habitable. Wroblewski seemed keen, and their boss Kowalow said that as long as he got his money, 'You can do what you like.' Socha also decided to make a proper job of the shaft. He looked over the piece of work again and suggested they could reinforce the walls with cement and, in the process, provide grips to make climbing in and out a little easier. He also suggested a way of disguising the entrance, by shaping it into a square. From his workshop he brought a standard iron grill and fitted it over the opening – making it seem like an official drain. Down in the chamber, a similar trap was added to the exit. Weiss, Kuba, Weinberg, Berestycki and Margulies all worked on improving the shaft. Margulies recalled. 'This is when I got to know Socha. Some of us were working from above, others were working from below, getting rid of the rubble.'

Margulies never saw anyone but Weiss, Berestycki and Socha during this period. So far as he was aware, there were no more than four or five people involved in the work. According to the Berestycki account, they took extraordinary precautions:

From the beginning, we all wore masks. They decided that they should only meet wearing masks; balaclavas, in fact. It was so that they would never be able to identify each other if forced. Socha was frightened and did not want to endanger his friends – and they also didn't know whether to trust each other.

As they laboured under Socha's direction, the team made long journeys through the sewers looking for a suitable hiding place. After about a week's search Socha found somewhere down the main chamber that might be suitable. Chiger and his colleagues had to take a look.

With Socha leading the way, his carbide lamp chasing back the darkness, they moved in single file down the pathway beside the Peltwa, one hand feeling the wall beside them. Every so often their progress was halted when the wall beside them abruptly disappeared into the entrance of a six-foot-high tunnel. At regular intervals, these great elliptical vomitories appeared, issuing a foot or so of water into the river. Here the ledge seemed to be cut away by the water rushing to the Peltwa, forcing the explorers to step down into the current, wade through it and climb back up on to the continuing ledge. Any slip as they crossed the gap, and they would be swept into the Peltwa.

Socha led them down-river, to a small stone bridge that arched across to the other side. From there they were led back up-river again to what appeared to be another elliptical tunnel. That was it. It looked, in every way, just like any of the other of the tunnels, except that no water flowed from it. Instead the waters from the Peltwa eddied in and out of the opening, soaking the soil at the bottom. It seemed as though the engineers had bored some fifteen or twenty metres into the earth, then changed their minds and bricked up the face. Halfway up the face was a narrow pipe emitting a gentle smear of water down the wall. The bottom was silted up with material that had been deposited during high tides, and it was alive with rats. Here was their sanctuary.

Very soon, Margulies, Weinberg and others had been introduced to Socha and were all pressed into whatever work was deemed necessary to prepare the tunnel for habitation. They took it in turns to come each day to clear away the soil and debris; the usual material that chokes an urban river. They brought down boards and constructed narrow benches that could be sat or slept upon. They also began storing provisions. Here, Margulies excelled himself. From his connections with shopkeepers and Ukrainian farmers, he collected quantities of cereals, barley, oats and flour, which he sealed in large glass jars. He got tins of pickled cucumbers, sugar and kerosine. Margulies ensured they had plenty of fuel for the small stove which they planned to bring down. He also managed to get hold of large quantities of carbide, to fuel the lamps the sewer workers carried with them everywhere. Everything was squirrelled away in a dozen different places.

During these trips back and forth from the sewer, Margulies had begun to notice a young girl who lived next door to the Weisses. 'I remember seeing Klara on the street one day. I thought she was very pretty,' he later reminisced. He began to take an interest, bringing her and Manya food and medicine.

Klara recalled: 'Suddenly, one day he's sitting in my room and talking. I suppose he came to see Mr Weiss. I didn't know anything at that time. I didn't know about any plan, or tunnel or what they were doing.' Margulies's visits became more regular and soon they had formed an attachment. Klara continued: 'I can't remember how we survived, my sister and I, before Mundek came along. We had no money, Manya had no work and was getting sick – and then he was there, wheeling and dealing.'

With each day Weiss and his group became more familiar with the chamber. Soon they were making journeys by themselves and taking the time to explore the new environment. Berestycki and Margulies wandered up one of the tunnels and discovered a pipe carrying fresh water. It cut across a tunnel at right-angles and was exposed for about two feet. With typical ingenuity, Berestycki plumbed a tap into the pipe for a constant supply of drinking water.

The most exhausting job was clearing the silt and mud from the floor of the tunnel, and the work was organized in shifts. Chiger, Berestycki and Weiss were on their way back to the shaft one afternoon, when they ran into the unexpected. Up ahead of them there was a glow from some lanterns. Strangers were approaching from the opposite direction. They turned and ran back towards the tunnel. They climbed inside and waited. Still the lanterns approached. They backed into the rear, pressing themselves against the wall. They could hear voices. Then someone called out, shouting to another a long way off.

'That's Wroblewski,' said Weiss.

Chiger moved to the entrance and peered round the edge. Wroblewski and Kowalow were striding towards them. Wroblewski called out again and waved his lantern above his head. They were virtually at the entrance to the tunnel, yet he was still calling at the top of his voice. Chiger heard a reply from the other direction and understood what was happening. Away in the distance another group of lights was approaching. Chiger returned to the others and explained what he'd seen. They listened to Wroblewski and Kowalow getting closer, step across the mouth of the tunnel, and continue, still calling to the others up ahead.

Eventually the men in the tunnel heard the two parties meet and start a conversation. Chiger decided to take another look to see what they were doing and moved back to the opening.

He seemed to be watching for ages.

'What are they doing?' asked Berestycki. Chiger moved back from the entrance.

'Coming back this way.'

Gradually the voices grew louder again. Three, four, perhaps five men altogether. Chiger and the others moved deep into the back of the tunnel, trying to make themselves as inconspicuous as possible. The lanterns flashed past them, as Wroblewski, Kowalow and the strangers waded across the opening – and continued away again. The three men at the end of the tunnel remained in their lair until they could hear nothing but the sound of the river. Then they made their way back to the cellar.

The following day Socha paid them a visit.

'You were all very lucky yesterday.'

'Wroblewski didn't see us. We hid in the tunnel.'

'Of course they saw you. That's why Wroblewski and Kowalow were there,' explained Socha.

'It doesn't make sense. They walked straight passed us.'

'Wroblewski knew that there would be another party of workers in that area, so they went down to watch out for them. They saw you on your way back to the cellar, realized that you had gone back into the tunnel and so just walked on past you to meet up with the other group.'

'What were the other group of workers doing there?'

Socha shook his head and took a deep breath. 'They had been ordered to escort some Germans to a spot not far from where you were working, to retrieve the body of an SS man that had been found hanging there. Some of your people had opened a manhole in the street, tied a piece of rope to the top rung of the ladder, put the other end round the German's neck and pushed him down the manhole.'

Action by the resistance was always a double-edged sword. While keeping alive the prospect of fighting back, it also brought down the wrath of the occupiers in its most terrible form. On this occasion they began with the execution of a dozen or so members of the Jewish police. They were taken to Loketka Street, amid scenes of indiscriminate butchery and lynched from the balconies of the houses there. This was expected to make the Jewish police more determined to maintain order amongst their compatriots. The following day, SS and Ukrainian militia raided the ghetto, sweeping away hundreds more to be executed.

With the sounds of boots and rifle fire echoing in the street outside the barrack, Weiss suddenly put his head round Klara's door. 'Come on, get your sister.'

Klara recalled: 'I had to drag Manya towards the opening. She had typhus and they were killing everybody who was sick.' Margulies, Klara and Manya, Weiss and his family and friends slipped down the hole into the cellar, put the boards back in place behind them and waited. They spent a day in the sewer, waiting for the *Aktion* to cease.

'For me I always remember that day, because I felt safe. It was like a small paradise, a safe place,' Klara remembered. But the experience had been terrifying for Manya. She got decidedly worse as the day wore on and had become almost hysterical with anxiety, struggling against Margulies and Weiss's attempts to keep her calm. Klara recalled her sister crying: 'I'd rather be dead, than stay there again.'

Chapter IV

On the evening of 31 May, Chiger, Berestycki and Kuba Leinwand slipped down the shaft to continue work on the tunnel they planned to make their home. Their anxiety was steadily rising and they knew that time was running out. They met with Socha that night to discuss their final plans.

While the meeting was taking place in the sewers, the authorities were hosting a concert out in the street near the administration block. The Julag orchestra was playing popular pieces for the few hundred who had turned up for a little distraction. In Chiger's account he wrote that in addition to the music: 'Grzymek arranged a play written by himself and invited everyone to attend the performance.' One of those at the concert was Halina Wind, the young woman who lived with Weiss and his mother. Throughout the evening, the music was heard drifting through the deserted streets.

Paulina had stayed in the cellar with her children, waiting for Chiger and the others to return. Just after eleven Paulina heard Halina's footsteps in the rooms above. She was breathless and apparently rushing from room to room. Paulina raised herself close to the floor boards in order to hear what was being said.

'This is it, the end. The Ukrainian militia and the Gestapo have already spread throughout the Julag. We have to escape,' Halina shouted. From out in the street came the sound of trucks pulling up outside and the rhythmic crump of boots; fifty, a hundred. three hundred – up and down the street.

By the time the men emerged from the sewer, the barrack was already in uproar. Chiger climbed into the room above and went to the window to look. Already standing there was a short, tough-looking character. Margulies tossed him the news.

'They're shooting the Jewish police. That's it, it's all finished now.'

They could see that the Gestapo and Ukrainian militia had herded together a group of terrified men wearing the plain peaked caps and dark armbands of the Jewish police. A few men lay dead at their feet. A Gestapo officer took hold of each man's cap and tossed it away. Likewise their belts and armbands were removed, and then as though it was all part of the same process, they were then each of them summarily shot on the spot. Some of them ran – or tried to run – and were cut down by machine-gun fire. The shooting of the Jewish police was the clearest signal yet. It could only mean the Julag would no longer function; the population was to be eliminated.

'Let's start packing,' said Margulies and he left for his room.

Chiger peered through the window. 'Everyone was in a state of panic. Running in every direction.'

Having seen enough, he moved back down to the cellar to confirm what his wife had already heard. She in the meantime was helping Kristina and Pawel get into their overcoats. Chiger began packing a knapsack and some bags with all the essentials they had thought they ought to take. Bandages, food, medicine, torches, candles.

Margulies had run across to the neighbouring barrack, where he lived. He climbed up through a trap in the ceiling and crawled through the attic to the water tank at one end. He reached behind and removed a revolver he had hidden there. He recalled: 'I bought it from a man in the ghetto long before, with some bullets. It had been taken from a Russian tank crew. Sometimes, during an *Aktion* at night, I used to fire at the Germans. No one would know where the shots were coming from. But it frightened people, so I kept it hidden.'

Margulies had no thoughts of fighting that night. His mind was concentrated on getting back under Weiss's floor. Out in the street the Gestapo had begun using heavy machine-guns. Bursts of heavy firing cut through the background of rising hysteria. The liquidation exercise, carried out by soldiers moving methodically through the ghetto, took hours. Accounts suggest that thousands were shot that night. Many insist that no one left the Julag alive. One witness claimed: 'They were just lined up against the wall and cut down. One group after another, like an assembly line. Those clearing the dead bodies could hardly keep up.'[4]

Meanwhile, amidst the utter confusion, there were horrifying scenes of families being cut down or torn apart as each member fought for his or her survival. And everywhere people were being shot. The gunfire went on, round after round.

'It was pitiful to watch. People running in every direction, they didn't know where they were going. It was utter chaos,' recalled Klara Keler. As she stood with Manya by the window in their room, Margulies came running in shouting, 'It's time to go down. Now!'

Klara looked across at her sister, who simply shook her head. Then the elderly Mrs Weiss and Halina appeared at the doorway.

'Come on, girls, don't wait.' The girls followed and met with

Berestycki. In Weiss's room, there seemed to be no sign of movement. Inside he and his wife stood silently opposite each other, his daughter clinging to her mother. Neither would move.

'We can't wait any longer.'

'I'm not going down there,' his wife shouted. She watched as people began to gather round the hole in their floor. The fear of imminent extinction did not seem to have affected her. She was not going to be persuaded, she was resolute.

Meanwhile, their room began to fill with strangers, people who had heard of some kind of tunnel. They brought with them fresh reports from the street. The Germans had begun to use flame throwers, moving through the streets sending bursts of fire into each shattered hovel until entire streets were ablaze. Stunned, mute with horror, they stumbled down into the cellar. Words couldn't describe what they had seen. It was death on a scale as yet unimagined. Some wept for release from the nightmare, while others, though terrified, kept going.

Having packed their provisions, Chiger set about marshalling his family towards the shaft. Everyone who had actually worked on the project knew what to expect, but their families and friends were soon horrified by the foul-smelling hole in the floor. Others had edged their way around the shaft, but were holding back from the unknown.

'I can't I can't do it,' someone screamed.

'Feet first, feet first!' Margulies was saying, trying not to raise his voice.

Meanwhile, Halina, Berestycki and old Mrs Weiss had also climbed down into the cellar. Halina looked across the cramped space and saw Paulina with her children for the first time. For an instant she was reminded of her own mother and some instinct moved her to stay close to the woman. Chiger was still shepherding his family to the opening, where they balked at the prospect. His brother-in-law Kuba was first to descend, to show how it was done. Then Paulina – '... someone pushed me from behind. I was pushed down through the shaft.'

Kristina and Pawel, already frightened by the stream of strangers pushing their way to the shaft, were determined not to follow. Kristina recalled with horror: 'I saw the entrance to some dark place. I didn't know what it was but it smelled terrible and my father said you have to go there.' She remembered struggling against her father's grip. 'I started to cry. I was scared and I said, "I don't want to go, Daddy!" And he said, "You must, Krisia, you must, please."'

His strong hands on her shoulders edged her forwards until there was no escape. With her father standing behind her, she slipped to the floor and was pushed from behind into the shaft. As she slid against the rough concrete she suddenly felt a pair of hands take hold of her ankles and pull her the rest of the way down – into her personal nightmare. 'It was total darkness and all I could hear was rushing water, like a waterfall – and screaming. I was terrified.'

In a moment Pawel was beside her and, eventually, her father. Back in Weiss's room, the situation had quickly deteriorated. Before anyone could have done anything about it, the place had become choked with people, some clutching a few belongings, most of them total strangers. They streamed down into the cellar, most of them completely ignorant of where they were going. There was nothing Margulies or the others could do but usher them towards the shaft.

'Don't stop, keep going down. Don't block up the hole!' cried Margulies. He and Berestycki knelt above the entrance, helping each one to edge their way down. Klara and her sister Manya finally reached Weiss's room. It was packed with people, struggling and fighting towards the hole in the floor. By the time the last of their friends had arrived, it was hopelessly chaotic and they knew it. All their preparations were in jeopardy. There was nothing they could do to stem the tide, except urge them to move more quickly down the shaft.

Outside, the night sky was filled with flames and clouds of swirling sparks, while the streets were littered with the dead. News arrived that a fleet of lorries had arrived and they were herding people aboard. A new wave of panic swept through the room. Down in the cellar, Margulies and Berestycki began shouting and man-handling people in an effort to quench the hysteria. They pushed them down the shaft and if they got stuck, stamped on their shoulders – anything to speed up the exodus. Then Weiss's wife burst out with some news.

'There's no need for this. They say we're going to be safe. They say they're going to take us somewhere where we will work – somewhere else – making clothes.'

'Who said?' asked Margulies from the cellar.

'Someone in the street,' she replied. 'We'll have rest and proper food and warm clothes to wear.'

'They are killing people in the street!' shouted Margulies. 'This is the end.'

He came up into the room and took hold of Klara's hand. She, in turn, held Manya's.

'Come now,' Margulies ordered.

'But Manya won't come.'

Margulies looked at Manya who was staring at the hole in the floor. She shook her head.

'I couldn't face it again. How long would we be down there?'

Manya asked. No one could tell her.

'Until the *Aktion* is over,' someone ventured.

'I won't go down there.'

Meanwhile Weiss and Berestycki had ushered old Mother Weiss and Halina towards the cellar. Weiss's wife and daughter stood apart, stony faced. Mrs Weiss looked across at the youthful Halina and then at her husband. For anyone who had noticed her expression, the implication was obvious. Besides, there had been arguments between Weiss and his wife ever since Halina had arrived at their house. Mrs Weiss was convinced that her husband was in love with the young woman.

'Why is she going down?'

'Everyone is going down.'

'You can't live in a sewer.'

The argument escalated, but no one wanted to intervene. It may seem extraordinary that just as their world was being engulfed in flames, a husband and wife might reach a crisis over a suspected infidelity. From all accounts, Mrs Weiss's suspicions were wholly unfounded. There was no such relationship between Weiss and Halina. Yet, living in an atmosphere of constant persecution, perhaps it's not surprising that deeply buried fears and anxieties had come to the surface.

While her son and daughter-in-law argued, old Mother Weiss and Halina climbed down into the cellar and were led by Berestycki into the shaft. They slipped down into the underworld. In Halina's account, she wrote, 'I heard something that sounded like a river. I saw a lot of people. Some held torches and some had candles.' Every so often, she heard the sound of a splash when someone slipped, or jumped into the river. Soon Berestycki descended too, took Halina by the hand and led her and old Mrs Weiss away.

'Our sewer workers will be here. Just come with me.'

She hadn't a clue what he meant, but she followed.

Meanwhile, in Weiss's room, Margulies still had hold of Klara's hand. His grip had become almost vice-like, wordlessly imploring 'I won't let you go. I'll look after you.'

Manya stood like a statue, unable to move. Then Margulies suddenly remembered a woman they had taken down on the previous occasion. A mother of two daughters. He told Klara to stay where she was and that he'd be back in a few minutes. He dashed down the corridor in search of the woman and her children. As he passed a window, he caught a glimpse of the scene outside. Some of the Jewish police who had escaped the initial slaughter were being chased towards the barrack. Were they seeking refuge amongst their erstwhile kinsmen? Margulies knew they could not be allowed anywhere near Weiss's room or the cellar beneath. If everyone didn't climb down the hole immediately, they risked leading the Germans to the shaft, and eventually those already down below.

He stumbled into the woman's room but stopped dead in his tracks. There, in a corner, the mother and her two daughters lay retching. The cyanide they had taken had all but completely flushed the life from their bodies. 'I just covered them up with a blanket – what could I do? – and closed the door.'

Back in Weiss's room, Margulies took hold of Klara's hand again. Time was now critical.

'The Jewish police are coming this way.'

Manya had become hysterical and began to scream.

'I want to live, I want to live!'

Around her the last remaining escapers had become infected with her hysteria and the final moments were lost in almost total panic. In order to regain control, Margulies had begun striking people before launching them down to the cellar. The final few were sent down and Margulies turned to Klara.

'Come, come, come....'

'He was pulling me one way and she was pulling in the other,' recalled Klara. But Manya was no match for Margulies's determination.

'Come!' he repeated. Klara, in a daze, stepped into the cellar and did not glance back. Margulies followed and heaved the stone into place, closing the hole in Weiss's floor. Manya was left behind. Then Marguiles led Klara to the shaft and told her to climb down it. He followed, pulling the iron grate into place.

Klara landed on the narrow ledge, took one or two tentative steps and suddenly felt her foot slip off the edge and into the water. Margulies's powerful hand instantly grabbed her arm and she felt his weight hauling her back against the wall. In the flashes of light that punctured the darkness, she saw the Peltwa rushing past her feet. They edged away from the shaft and away from the terror of the exterminations.

Her first impression was of the terrible level of noise. The thundering river, coupled with the screams of those carried away in its current. Her instinct was to escape, to return to the air above, to the light. But there was Margulies almost dragging her along the ledge. The most shocking aspect of this new environment, the one which most disorientated Klara, was the crush of bodies: 'So many people – pushing, screaming, yelling to each other.'

The ledge was teaming with scores of people. Some were huddled in small groups, some were sliding along the wall, others were rushing – running and colliding with one another. Screams echoed up and down the chamber until the stones seemed to be vibrating with the noise. Where had they all come from? Most of them had lifted manholes in the street above and had found the simplest way down. They were doing the same thing that had happened at Warsaw and Lubin. Using the sewers as the most obvious escape out, now that the ghetto was an inferno. It was pointless. The Germans had already posted men at every manhole in the city, waiting for anyone to emerge. There would be no escape. Klara felt swamped by the panic.

'Stay by the wall,' Margulies shouted at the people around him. 'Don't run!' But it was useless.

The chamber was also filled with torches and candles which created a terrifying, instant tableau of tortured faces captured in momentary flashes of light. Margulies remembered the vain attempts to help those in the water: 'Every so often you heard a splash as someone slipped off the edge into the water. You heard them scream, but it was too late. We had two ropes and I threw each one to someone in the water. But the current was too fast, it just took the rope.' They were simply swept away by the torrent, and the tug on the rope forced them to let go. The sides were smooth with slime and offered virtually no purchase. It was soon apparent that once someone was in the water, there was nothing you could do.

On and on came the waves of bodies along the ledge, while Margulies and Klara fought against the tide. Out of the midst walked Mr Katz. Everyone knew him, he had once owned a fashionable shoe shop on the Teodor Platz, not far from the opera house. Out of his pocket he took a white handkerchief, which he held out before him.

'Save me. Save me.'

Margulies watched him. 'What can I do?'

Katz opened the handkerchief and, in the occasional flashes of light, was the unmistakable glint of diamonds.

'Save me. Please,' he cried as he proffered the handkerchief before him. 'Take me with, take me with …!'

'Where can I take you with …?'

Suddenly Katz lunged forward, then sideways as someone rushed past. Katz and the diamonds disappeared. His cries and thrashing in the water continued for a moment, but were soon lost in the noise.

The chamber resounded with screams. It was bedlam and there seemed to be no way to defuse the panic and the forward surge of the mass. The people had no idea where they were going, just forward, forward. For some, the waters were a form of escape and they leapt willingly into the river, to be carried away by the current. Others stopped and sat quietly on the bank and simply pushed themselves into the dark waters. Less than a kilometre down the tunnel they would emerge into the moon-light. If they had not already drowned, they would be picked off by the soldiers posted at the mouth of the Peltwa armed with powerful lights and sub-machine-guns.

When Paulina Chiger stepped into the chamber she was horri-fied. She was trapped on the narrow ledge finding it impossible to stand still and take everything in.

'I had two bags, which I gave to Kuba. He put them down on the ledge and they slipped straight into the river. All my packing, gone straight away. I had hold of the two children beside me. We had to cling on to the damp wall and with the rushing noise of the water and the total darkness – it left a terrible impression on me.'

Kuba, Chiger's brother, felt terrible about losing the bags, but there was nothing he could do. He stood close by, helping to protect the children from injury. Chiger stood a little way apart, trying to orientate himself. He was hoping in vain that they might make contact with Socha. From behind came an apparently endless stream of people emerging from the shaft. Everything seemed lost, on the verge of disaster. 'We moved slowly along the ledge. My husband and Kuba leading the way,' recalled Paulina.

Like everyone else they were pushed forward by the force of the crowd. Fear had become infectious. Chiger had never imagined the panic would have been so great. He became convinced they would be forced towards their certain death. Kuba moved in front of them, trying to maintain some purpose in their flight. He barrelled his way forward, glancing back over his shoulder to the others, then his face was gone. He had slipped, his foot went over the ledge and he was quickly up to his shoulders in water. Chiger lunged forward to grab him and found Kuba's flailing arm. In his move to reach his brother, the knapsack filled with provisions heaved up over his head and into the water. It was gone. Meanwhile, Kuba was clawed out of the water. 'As our provisions floated away, we stood there, pushed and jostled by screaming people, all trying, fighting for first place in the rush – to where?' Chiger wrote.

Chiger, Kuba, Paulina and the children then continued wrestling their way along the ledge. Kristina was on her father's back, clinging tightly round his neck. Pawel was in Paulina's arms.

'How long must we go here, how long, Daddy?' Kristina cried again and again, while her father tried to keep up his gentle reassurances. They approached the familiar stone bridge that led across to the other ledge. It was the only way to the shelter they had spent weeks preparing. But now they were surrounded by a sea of terrified people and Chiger realized that if they tried to cross it would probably encourage everyone else to follow. All their work to create somewhere secret would be lost. All their hopes seemed to plunge to nothing as they were carried relentlessly on past the bridge, past their sanctuary.

Meanwhile, the other group was much further ahead. Halina had clung tenaciously to Berestycki's hand once she had descended on to the ledge. Old Mrs Weiss stood her ground, while the tide of people passed by. Her son joined them a little later, without his wife and daughter. With Weiss clinging to his mother and Halina clutching Berestycki, they edged along in search of a familiar face, buffeting their way along. Occasionally they would come to the entrance of a tunnel. Down these tunnels there might be the faintest beam of light from an opened manhole above, dimly illuminating some wretched group huddled together, or struggling along against water flowing knee-deep. Suddenly, Berestycki was blinded by the fierce beam of a carbide lamp. For an instant they had no idea whether it meant death or rescue. It was rescue. It was Socha.

'Where are the others?' he shouted.

They looked around them and shrugged. Socha led them along the ledge and eventually to a shelter on the other side of the river. There he bade them wait as he and the light disappeared again.

Margulies and Klara struggled along, someway behind the Chigers. They saw no sign of Jacob, Weiss or any of the others. When they eventually got to the bridge, they made their way across to the other side and towards the entrance to the shelter. When they got there, it was filled with people. A doctor, one of Weiss's neighbours, had led a group of people to the tunnel and established themselves there. There was no one they recognized, so Margulies moved on.

Eventually, the Chigers were able to come to a halt some way further down. The crowd seemed to have thinned out, and they were able to turn and move back in the opposite direction. Feeling their way along the wall, keeping as far as possible from the water, they eventually stumbled into another opening. Paulina recalled: 'It seemed like a cave and was draped in sheets of cobwebs. We stepped inside and our feet plunged into mud. Around our legs scuttled unseen rats.' They clung to each other, trying not to scream as dozens of tiny feet and tails lashed against their legs. 'There we stood with a small flickering candle, frightened and lost.'

There was Chiger, Paulina, Kristina, Pawel, and Kuba; all of them clutching each other and trying to catch their breath. As they whispered to each other inspiring hope and courage, the noise around them seemed to abate. They sat on their haunches and tried to regain control of their senses. But they were shaken from this brief respite by the sounds of gunfire and explosions. Then more screaming. As someone ran hysterically past the cave, the Chigers heard them cry something about grenades.

'The Germans are lifting the manholes and throwing down grenades.'

Kuba stepped out on to the ledge to look.

'What is it?'

'What about the others? Weiss and the others?' Kuba took a few steps down the ledge. 'I'll go look for them.'

'Wait!' Chiger called, but he was gone. Chiger watched him disappear. The little family sat and waited, and the time passed slowly. After some time Kuba and the others had still not returned. As Chiger and Paulina began to wonder if they would ever see them again, the sound of Kuba's cries suddenly echoed down the chamber. Chiger grabbed the candle and stepped out on to the ledge.

'I won't be long. It's Kuba,' he said as he departed.

Now Paulina and the children were stranded on their own. They huddled together and waited. 'It might have been a few minutes, it might have been an hour,' recalled Paulina. Time was elastic. The two children nestled deeper into their mother's warmth, waiting for their father's familiar shape at the entrance. In the darkness, it was difficult to control their imaginations. The most terrible spectres emerged from the damp ooze around their feet and the clinging films above their heads. Paulina watched the glinting eyes of the rats watching her. As time began to work upon her reason, she finally heaved a deep sigh and spoke to her children.

'Krisia, I don't have a husband, you don't have a father any more. We have to leave here. I can't sit here with the rats any longer, we're going out again.'

The three of them emerged from the cave and stumbled along the ledge. Paulina struggled with a child in each hand. Every so often, they had to stop when Krisia, walking on the outside, slipped off the edge into the water and had to be hauled back up again. They paused against the wall to catch their breath, then continued. She had no idea which direction to take so they just walked on. 'And I thought to myself, whoever meets us here, even the Gestapo, let them get me out!' recalled Paulina.

Suddenly Kristina saw up ahead a flash of light. Then she saw it again.

'It's Daddy. It's Daddy!' She was so terrified, the sound came instinctively. The light turned on them and began to grow brighter.

'It's Daddy. It's Daddy,' she repeated. They stumbled forward.

Paulina thought, 'towards salvation, or death, if necessary.' Kristina was in no doubt, it was towards her father.

'Daddy!'

'Krisia! Pepa!' It was Chiger's voice. He was upon them, they embraced.

'How did you get here?' His voice was mixed with anger and relief.

'We walked. I thought we were abandoned,' Paulina explained.

'But you walked all this way – with the children? You should not have left that place, it's too dangerous.'

'I didn't even know if you were alive!' Paulina countered.

As they stood together not knowing whether to embrace or be angry, Paulina noticed Kuba soaked to the skin.

'I pulled him out of the water again. At first I couldn't see him, and so I just walked in the direction of his cries. I held my candle aloft, and shielding its flare, saw him clinging to the side. I took off my belt and threw it to him and, after two or three attempts, he grabbed the end and I pulled him out.'

Reunited, the five turned and made their way back to the little cave. Inside once more, they sat there 'waiting for a miracle'.

'Where is Socha?' Chiger kept repeating. 'I saw him just this evening.'

Then they saw the approaching glare of a carbide lamp. It was Berestycki, searching the Peltwa chamber.

'Chiger?'

'Jacob! Jacob!' called Chiger. He vividly remembered the relief at meeting his friend again: 'We were overwhelmed with joy. At last a familiar face.'

Berestycki put his head inside the cave. 'Socha's just up ahead, he says you're to follow me and bring the children. He doesn't want to do anything without you.'

Within minutes they were reunited with Socha and the party continued towards their sanctuary.

'We have to go a separate way, to avoid all the people.' Socha led them to the opening to a narrow pipe at about head height, from which water poured into the Peltwa. Beneath it were a number of iron rungs set into the wall. Socha led the way and the others climbed after him, drenching themselves in the cascade. Later Paulina remembered how incongruous her thoughts had been at that moment:

> I had put the children into their woollen underwear, winter clothes, boots and overcoats to keep them warm in the cellar. Now everything was soaked, including the children's felt boots. Everything was now filled with water and they would all become so heavy. How would they ever get dry again?

They moved down the narrow pipe, struggling against the flow of water, and then turned into another pipe. They followed this a little way and emerged through the rear wall, into another of the elliptical tunnels. They were safe. 'After that, I was certain that he would be our guardian, that he would look after us,' was one of the few positive thoughts Paulina could recall from those hours.

Chiger had never ventured this far into the sewers and found it completely disorientating. He was equally dismayed when, once they were all inside, he realized they were not alone. Indeed, it was filled with people.

In an attempt to lighten the atmosphere, Socha proudly explained that they were at present situated directly beneath a market place. During the day they would be able to hear the traders arrive and set up their stalls. It all seemed rather odd information at that moment. They shuffled around, stepping over limbs and feeling for a space to sit. Paulina and the children squeezed into a damp space on the floor, Berestycki sat next to Kristina. On the other side of Paulina, a young girl took hold of Paulina's arm and squeezed it tightly. It was Klara Keler, who later recalled: 'I suddenly realized I was clutching Mrs Chiger's hand. I squeezed her so tightly I think she was black and blue.'

Klara had been led to the evil-smelling domain by Margulies, seated beside her. She sat amongst this maze of limbs and feet, while the last few moments with her sister played over and over in her mind. Somewhere amongst all the shapes were old Mrs Weiss, her son and the young girl Halina. Suddenly, everything became quite still. There were some seventy or more gathered in that space, each one isolated within their own thoughts and fears.

Chapter V

They sat upon black, unyielding silt that had built up in the tunnel. Gathered from hills to the south, the rich dark loam that supported the neighbouring villages of Bielosko and Snopkow was carried away in the waters of the Peltwa to be deposited against the walls of the sewers. Now it provided a floor that oozed dark moisture when a foot or hand pressed upon it. In that dank hole, a host of breathless souls whispered soothing messages to each other. They knew that for the time being at least, they had been saved. Three or four candles etched out groups of faces gloomily peering out of the darkness like images from an old Dutch master. Some heads were thrown back against the stone, staring into the middle distance, others coughed loudly, while some cradled their loved ones and tried to comfort them. As Chiger recalled, '... each was occupied in his own thoughts. How would this end? How will we survive? What was our fate?'

Above the muffled roar of the river, there came the sound of movement. The shuffle of someone moving down the pipe towards them. A blazing carbide lamp flooded in, seeming to populate the space with faces and shapes that had not been there before. As Socha fanned the light across the blinded faces, no one made a sound. All that could be heard was the soft hiss of the lamp as he moved amongst the feet and limbs.

Chiger saw the lamp illuminate Socha's own face, now creased with worry.

'What is it?'

He shook his head. 'There are maybe a hundred people scattered about, here and nearby.'

'What will you do?'

Socha shrugged. 'I don't know. I said we would help you and your family. The rest …'

These hundred or so survivors accounted for a fraction of the numbers that had escaped to the sewers. The total had been closer to four or five hundred, most of whom had perished in the Peltwa or returned to the surface where they were captured. According to Chiger's account, there were more than seventy gathered with them or nearby.

'I've just been up to the street.' Again a shake of the head.

'And …?'

'Everything on fire – still burning. So many dead.' The images he had seen in the street remained with him for the rest of his life. It became apparent to those who knew him that what he had witnessed that night had shaken his most fundamental beliefs. He seemed to be a man who approached matters with an inherent optimism, yet he had seen things that would have darkened anyone's soul. It weighed upon him and threatened to break the man at a time when the fugitives were depending upon him most. He was exhausted, too exhausted to do anything about it then and there. It would soon be dawn and he badly needed to sleep. He took another look at the crowd and then turned back to speak to Chiger.

'I'll be back in the morning with some food,' he said. Then he crept out again and left them to their thoughts.

In the re-darkened space, the silence was chilling. Somehow, the atmosphere had become harder to breath. In fact the air had become stifling.

'Blow out the candles. They are eating up the air,' said Chiger.

'I need to see.'

'What is there to see? There is nothing. Blow them out.'

Klara clutched Mrs Chiger's hand in hers. She had heard Socha say something about an agreement to save 'some people'. She couldn't bear to think about the prospect and contented herself with Paulina's hand. On the other side, young Krisia, exhausted like the others, dozed against the shoulder nearest to her. She was suddenly jerked awake by Berestycki, wrenching his arm away.

'Why are you so heavy? You're so small, but you're so heavy. I can't carry you.' In Berestycki's voice, one of the most amiable of souls, there were perhaps the first notes of irritation that threatened to affect everyone. The twin spirits of fear and suspicion were easily the most deadly infection to flourish in that domain and threaten the group's chances of survival.

Sleep came in brief snatches for some, others remained alert for some imminent catastrophe. The hours passed by grudgingly and as they did, the struggle to suppress their fears became more difficult. What gnawed away at them constantly was the sense of absolute helplessness.

Margulies recalled someone voicing their anxiety: 'To be at the mercy of those *goyim*, who might all become heroes by simply bringing the Germans on an expedition through the sewers.' Fears spread swiftly. Most of them had not the faintest idea who Socha was. The only logical reason why he should return was the lure of money. Nazi law was clear: whoever handed over Jews in hiding was rewarded with whatever wealth was captured with them. Either way, there seemed no reasonable way to sustain hope. Only a few clung to their conviction that Socha could be trusted, when logic dictated otherwise.

The following morning, Socha returned with his softly hissing lamp. With him he carried two workmen's bags, normally weighed down with rough heavy tools, but that morning they were filled with bread and potatoes. With this he planned to feed the multitude, passing out fists of torn bread. He had visited the other groups scattered around and done what he could with the food that he'd brought. There was no ceremony, no gasps of gratitude as he arrived. The food was simply passed around in complete silence.

This manna brought about a transformation of feelings. The sense of embattled hopelessness subsided. Chiger asked about what was happening. Any report from the street was eagerly devoured in the hope that it might dispel the nightmare. The prospect of news was almost as nourishing as the food he brought. But at the moment, though burdened with knowledge, Socha found it hard to deliver. What he said confirmed their worst fears. His description banished all hope that they might have been wrong about the German intensions.

'We saw terrible things. The ghetto was set on fire. Everything. The shooting went on all night and still now it goes on. They rounded up ten, twenty people at a time, stood them against a wall and shot them. Then they brought in trucks, loaded up the bodies, took them somewhere outside the city and returned for another load.'

In his book, *The Death Brigade*, Leon Wells described being transported from the ghetto. Wells was a friend of Berestycki's and had been tempted to hide with him in the sewers, but at the last moment decided against it.

SS commandos drove men, women and children in front of them. Most of us were calm and composed; many women were singing. We were loaded on tram trucks and taken to the Janowska camp. There we were herded into the parade ground, the last gathering place of so many thousands. We remained there for a day and a night, guarded by the SS. At night searchlights were trained upon us.[5]

Not everyone had left calmly, singing as they were herded into the waggons. A large number had hidden themselves in the very fabric of the buildings. The man who supervised the *Aktion* was SS General Katzmann, who wrote five weeks after the event:

The Jews tried every means to evade evacuation. They not only attempted to escape from the ghetto, but hid in every imaginable corner, in pipes, in chimneys, in sewers and canals. They built tunnels under the hallways, underground; they widened cellars and turned them into passageways; they dug trenches underground and cunningly created hiding places in lofts, woodsheds, attics and inside furniture ... we were compelled, therefore, to act brutally from the beginning in order to avoid sustaining greater casualties among our men. We had to blast and burn many houses.'[6]

There had also been many prepared to resist with arms. Socha and those in the sewers would probably never have heard about it. In the building that had housed the bakery was:

... a team of young men, who had sworn not to be taken

alive. They were well armed with automatic weapons they had bought from Rumanian soldiers who had passed through Lvov on their way to the front. When the Germans uncovered the bunker they were hidden in, yelling '*Juden Raus!*' and waited for a few Jews to come ... they left through a reserve exit and began mowing down the startled SS and Ukrainians. Alarmed by the resistance, the Germans called for reinforcements and an overwhelming SS force arrived. In a prolonged battle, they shot and killed twice as many Germans as their own number.'[7]

In contrast, Socha's account was bleak and unrelenting.

It still goes on. Hundreds, thousands are dead. Like a machine, they work their way through, searching for life. In any inaccessible corner, they simply toss in grenades. Many were taken alive in the tram waggons, down the track to the Janowska camp.' Everyone knew the fate of the rest. They'd heard about the killings at the Janowska camp, and they had watched the trains to Belzec for over a year.

Inside the camp, many thousands were assembled on the parade ground and made to stand there for days. At irregular intervals, the SS would order certain age groups to step forward, then the victims were made to undress and were led away. The process continued until there were less than 400 men and women between the ages of fourteen and thirty. These would be put to work in the camp and were marched off to the barracks.[8]

Meanwhile, Socha continued, 'We were ordered to stay out of the sewers while they lifted the manhole covers and sprayed everyone with machine-guns and grenades. They even want to conduct patrols through the tunnels in search of any survivors. They've done this before. They simply stand at the end of the tunnel with flame throwers and no one can escape.'

The thought terrified everyone.

'I think the Jews out at the airfield working for the Luftwaffe are still alive. And some of the other camps, perhaps. I don't know.'

According to Chiger, Socha's description had a deeply shocking affect on all of them. They listened as he went on to describe one horror after another, but they paid particular attention to the facts about the Germans making patrols of the sewers.

'That won't be a problem. Kowalow normally puts me in charge. I know where to take them and where not. They won't find you – but it is something that has to be done. It may go on for some weeks, but I'll tell you everything.'

They devised certain warning signals, should anyone be strolling about the tunnels when a patrol was about. If they saw Socha's lamp and he could be seen to be rotating it slowly in a wide circular movement, then it meant he was not with the Germans and it was safe to approach. If not, they were to return as quickly as possible to their hiding place and Socha would ensure the Germans came nowhere near them.

In his absence, thoughts turned to his description of the scenes in the ghetto. Had their families survived and been amongst the ones taken to the Janowska camp? Isolated with their separate memories, a sullen hush settled on them all. Klara was constantly reminded of her sister Manya, whom she last saw in Weiss's room. Would she survive for long if they discovered she had typhus?

Margulies's thoughts were for his brothers with whom he had lost touch months before. Weiss thought of his wife and how tragic it was to have parted in anger. So they passed the time.

Occasionally a voice would call, 'Is Ruth here?'

'Is Rothfeld there?'

'Is there a Feldman here?'

This way, an unofficial roll-call was taken. The two engineers who had worked on the project from the outset were not present. 'They're dead now. They never came down, they were taken away,' recalled Margulies.

The following few days passed slowly, marked only by the arrival of Socha and Wroblewski laden with food. Each time Socha turned up, it was clear he was overwhelmed by the vastness of his task. Something would have to be done, but he hardly knew what. Despite the money he was paid, it was still beyond him to gather enough food to feed so many people. In his absence, speculation was rife. How could he buy so much food without raising suspicion? How long would their money last? How long would they need to stay there? What already seemed clear was that their present accommodation would not be practical as a long-term shelter. There was hardly room to move, no one could sleep stretched out, the walls were perpetually running with water, the floor a sludge of dark filth.

Some seemed to accept the reality of the situation swiftly, and were content to sit there and simply get accustomed to the noises of the tunnels: interminable echoes broken occasionally by what they thought were gunshots or explosions, the constant roar of the Peltwa in the main chamber, and during the day, the incongruous sounds of street vendors floated down from the market overhead.

Just as Socha had predicted, the neighbouring tunnels were invaded by a German patrol. Orders shouted, the thunder of boots, cries of their victims – and the gunshots that seemed to echo endlessly. They sat frozen with fear in their little cavern, waiting to be discovered. Inevitably the danger drew nearer. 'We could hear the Germans shouting as they ran through the neighbouring pipe, searching amongst corpses for fugitives,' Chiger recorded. 'It was absurd; amidst all that, we could still hear the voices of street vendors, trying to sell their merchandise.'

The hunters never arrived.

Nevertheless, it was a brave man who ventured out to explore their domain. Berestycki and Margulies realized they could not always depend upon Socha to bring them water. They would have to fetch it for themselves. A number of water pipes appeared here and there throughout the system and they found the one to which Berestycki had ingeniously fitted a tap weeks before. Socha also discovered, at a spot that was much nearer to the group, a crack in a pipe that trickled fresh water. To collect the water, however, was a slow and tedious operation. A piece of cloth had to be wedged into the crack to direct the trickle of water into their jug. It took more than an hour to collect enough to have made a trip worthwhile.

*   *   *

On the fourth day, Socha arrived with his food and wanted to talk about the situation. There was no question about it, an obligation towards seventy or more people was overwhelming both him and Wroblewski. He felt like throwing it all in. Instead he decided to discuss the situation with Weiss and the others. The accounts vary as to how they arrived at a solution, but eventually it became clear what had to be done. According to Chiger: 'Socha agreed to go on, but only with a smaller group. He would lead it to where he and his colleagues had found a place in which a dozen or so people could live.'

He wanted them to make their own selection; those who could best afford to pay for their food and protection, who could be trusted, and perhaps more importantly, those who could form a cohesive group. The rest would have to survive as best they could on their own.

The moment Socha left, the group descended into acrimony as each in turn argued that they had the means to pay for their keep. It was an impossible situation for Weiss to arbitrate. Of course, he knew that he and his immediate colleagues would make up the core of a smaller group. The Chigers would also be included because it was known that they had means. But money would not be the only factor. Weiss had many friends, all of whom looked to him for salvation. Yet Socha had implied that it had to be a group of no more than twelve, if they were to have any chance of surviving.

Relatively little has been recorded of how the little group was selected. Chiger described the debate simply as 'a great deal of commotion'. There were arguments as to everyone's suitability, their character, and what they could or could not contribute. By the following day, when Socha returned, they had made a final selection numbering more than fifteen. Weiss, his core of friends, and the Chigers, including Kuba, had selected themselves. The rest had become desperate. Klara Keler had taken hold of Paulina's arm and proclaimed, 'You are my mother now!' She had no other words to express herself. She was completely at their mercy. She was such an unlikely candidate; a single girl without the means to pay for her survival. 'I didn't have anything, not even a handkerchief. Just my coat and what I stood in. So I didn't have much, just Mundek, who always kept very close to me.'

Her only other ally was Paulina, whom she clung to: '… begging Pepa to let her stay with the family.' According to Chiger, '… my wife succeeded in convincing Socha to let her stay and Klara did indeed look upon my wife as a mother.'

75

Socha noticed that though Margulies had been involved from the beginning, he had not been chosen. Socha had got to know Margulies during the work on the shaft and had no doubts.

'Take Margulies, you will need him,' he said.

Weiss had said nothing about Margulies, and Chiger knew nothing about him or his involvement in the project. As far as he was concerned, Margulies was simply '… a barber by profession and a trickster by disposition … [who] had been brought by Socha with some others … and had attached themselves almost forcefully, begging us to include them in our group.'

Inevitably the selection process generated a great deal of resentment and it is at this point in his account that Chiger first mentions his doubts about Weiss. He queried, 'Why had Weiss abandoned his wife and daughter … [and yet brought with him] a young girl – Halina, another woman and his friends the Weinbergs and the Orenbach brothers?' He had known nothing about the scene in the cellar between Weiss and his wife, nor what Weiss's feelings might have been after losing his family. Curiously, no one seemed to have enlightened him.

It was also around this time that Paulina first encountered Genia Weinberg.

'You bring children down here? Are you crazy?' she said to Paulina. 'What do you think you're doing? Are you crazy?' she kept repeating.

Paulina returned, 'What else can I do? Do you expect me to take them up to the street and leave them there? What do you think?'

A nerve had been exposed, not in Paulina but in Mrs Weinberg. She and her husband were two, but the Chigers, including Kuba, were five. Mrs Weinberg also had children, but they were elsewhere now. After the final count, there were twenty-one selected to leave the main group and follow Socha. 'It was very sad, but what could he do? He just couldn't cope with all those people,' recalled Paulina.

There are no other descriptions of their departure from the rest. With Socha in the lead, they proceeded down towards the main chamber. 'Walking along the ledge, our group resembled a cavalcade of marching ghosts, led by Socha's glimmering lamp. In the middle, Stefak Wroblewski strode with his lamp. It seemed an endless journey,' wrote Chiger.

Every fifty metres or so, their progress was halted at the large elliptical tunnels that emptied into the Peltwa. One by one, they had to step down into the rushing water and stride across to where the ledge continued. It would have been so easy to slip in the current and be carried sideways into the river. From the head of the cavalcade, Socha was sending words of warning back along the line.

They turned into one of the elliptical tunnels and proceeded away from the Peltwa. These tunnels, perhaps seven foot high, carried water usually up to about knee depth, but as the group was so tightly bunched down this route, they held up the flow of sewage so that it rose almost to hip level.

They walked on and on, travelling under one city block after another. For most of the travellers, it was their first real opportunity to explore the tunnels. 'It was just like an underground city – an underground Lvov,' recalled Paulina. 'Every house, every street had its own outlet to the system.'

Regularly drenched by unseen cascades from above, they were finally brought to a halt beneath a steel hatch that was bolted shut. Socha opened it and immediately let escape yet another deluge upon their heads. When the flow had subsided, he climbed through. Wroblewski stood beneath and helped each one up to Socha's outstretched hand, until they had all climbed through the hatch. The next pipe was some four feet high and necessitated crawling on all fours until eventually they arrived at a much larger tunnel which broadened out into a massive alcove strewn with large, crudely hewn limestone blocks, left over from the construction of the central chamber.

'This,' claimed Socha, 'is much more convenient and safer too.'

Exhausted, they staggered about the cavern, looking for somewhere they could stretch out and rest themselves. There was nowhere. Cold and drenched to the skin, they sat on the limestone blocks, gradually surveying their new home. It was dreadful. A cold, damp draft swept over their heads, and at times it whipped up into a fair wind. It howled and whistled through some unseen crack. At their feet, a trench carried a constant flow and rising from it was the unmistakable stench of raw sewage.

'We are right beneath the Church of Our Lady of the Snows,' Socha announced, as though their proximity to a place of worship would in some way compensate for the smell of excrement. It seemed that the place he had brought them to was somehow in the foundations of the church. There were municipal toilets in a square nearby, which had been a public disgrace – even above the ground. Every time the toilets were flushed a new wave of excrement passed down the trench and sometimes overflowed across the floor. They settled down on the stones, shivering in a howling wind, while rats scuttled about their feet. So, here was their first home in the sewers: cold, wet, and reeking of shit.

Chapter VI

They calculated that they were only about twelve feet beneath the Church of Our Lady of the Snows. They could hear the daily visits of worshippers and even the murmuring of prayers. The conduit for these sounds was a steel waste pipe, the top half of which was covered only by a wire mesh, and which passed through their space on its way to the waters of the Peltwa. As the pipe seemed to be such an efficient sound conductor, they consequently believed that their own voices would be amplified back through the same pipe and heard coming up through the drains in the church. So they resolved to talk only in whispers.

Each day, Socha arrived with food and, if possible, he brought drinking water too which was shared out amongst the group. Despite this regular supply of food and water, their environment was squalid and many of them soon succumbed to dysentery. The children were the first. Though crippled with diarrhoea, there was little privacy and they were obliged to relieve themselves in a corner of the room. With the regular loss of fluid, they became seriously dehydrated. Fresh drinking water became the most precious commodity and the very limited quantities that could be brought were carefully rationed. The allowance was about half a cup of water per person. Chiger and Paulina refused their rations and passed them on to their children.

'The dampness in the air was enough for us; we took it in through the pores of our skin,' recalled Paulina.

The morale of the group plunged further. They huddled together on the cluster of crudely hewn limestone blocks, trying to avoid the chilling draft that cut through the place. The Chigers cradled their children on their laps, whispering comforting words to them. They slept that way too. There was no space to lie down and so everyone huddled into groups, exploring every possible angle into which they could squeeze their limbs. Soon everyone had dysentery and were racked with painful stomach cramps and diarrhoea. 'We had a shovel and every so often Margulies would scrape the shit into the trough,' recalled Paulina.

They became so thirsty that Chiger and some others drank the sewer water and inevitably became chronically ill. They had lost the stove they had planned to bring with them, so there was no means of boiling the water. He asked Socha if he could bring some alcohol on his next visit, and perhaps an empty tin. He planned to try to improvise a stove. He poured the alcohol into an empty sardine tin, and set it alight. Over the tiny flame he held a cup of water which he boiled and then gave to Krisia and Pawel with a lump of sugar.

In the cavern beneath the church, some of the group set about trying to make the conditions more comfortable. Margulies, Berestycki and Chaskiel Orenbach took the initiative, found their way down to the main chamber and set out on the long walk back towards the ghetto. They passed the same ledges and tunnels, that, less than a fortnight before, had been crowded with desperate people. As they moved forward, they heard nothing but their own footsteps mixed with the roar of the Peltwa. The cries and echoes of all the people who had followed them into the sewers had ceased long ago.

Their journey would take them past the tunnel they had prepared before the liquidation. All their labour spent clearing the debris and constructing benches had been for nothing. The tunnel had been occupied by strangers long before they had arrived. Margulies recalled struggling past the opening, on that first dreadful night, and finding the place full. Now, as he and the others made their first journey back that way, he wondered if they were still there and how they were coping.

As they stepped into the entrance they saw what they'd expected. Some twenty-six people, huddled in the darkness, some way down the tunnel. This forlorn group, led by a doctor, had all come from the barrack and must have been encouraged to come down by Weiss. They tossed a greeting to each other, but there was little else they could have done. Margulies recognized a few faces. He recalled: 'They were all seated on the benches we had made. We let them stay there. We couldn't have looked after them, but we knew they were there.'

Margulies and the others had not come to pay a visit. They were going further. They had decided to return to Weiss's cellar, partly to satisfy their curiosity but mostly to scavenge for anything that might make their existence more bearable. They planned to get back into the barrack, where there might be something that could be salvaged.

As they approached the spot where the shaft broke through the chamber roof, it seemed both familiar and strange. So much had happened since the night of the liquidation. When they peered back up through the shaft, they could feel a soft draft of fresh air against their faces. It was deceptively peaceful. It was

81

also completely quiet. They climbed towards the draft and miraculously, the iron grate was still in place. If the Germans had got down to the cellar, then they had discovered nothing more curious than a simple drain in the floor. However, as well as the grate, there was the stone slab which Margulies had heaved into the hole in Weiss's floor. The real test would be shifting the slab.

When they were all inside the cellar, they heaved against the slab, raising it a few centimetres. The light in the room nearly blinded them, yet the lights were off and it was late in the evening. They had already grown accustomed to the dark. When their eyes had settled, they looked again. The place was deserted. Nothing moved. They shifted the slab out of the way and climbed into the room. Everything was in utter ruin. Furniture was shattered, clothes had been ripped into rags, broken plates crunched under their feet. There was nothing worth salvaging and they knew they would have to move on. A wind outside was swinging a window on its hinges, but otherwise, it was silent. Every step they took seemed to announce their presence to the entire district.

To get into any of the other rooms they had to step out into the corridor that ran the full length of the building. If there was anyone on guard, there would be nowhere to hide, no escape. Gathering all their courage, they peered round the door. The corridor was deserted.

There had been nearly a hundred families living in the rooms on either side and the corridors had once teemed with children. It had never been as silent as it was that evening. Margulies crossed to another room and looked out across Peltewna Street. More desolation. The buildings opposite had been gutted by fire. They were roped off and patrolled by Ukrainian guards. It would have been suicide to step out into the street. Moving as quietly as possible from room to room, they found some plates, cups, a tea pot, some tin bowls, some bed linen and a pillow. And one grand discovery: Berestycki laid his hands on a small kerosine stove. They didn't search far; they didn't want to force their luck, and there would be another time. From the window, Margulies could see the Ukrainian guards looting the building across the way. They had brought their families to help. Children were stumbling under the weight of suitcases filled with plunder. Having gathered up their own booty, Margulies and the others slipped back into the cellar and were about to slide the slab back into place, when they heard a noise. They froze and waited. It was the sound of breathing and then a slow, weak shuffle. Whoever it was seemed to be unaware of their presence. Margulies stepped towards the sound and there was a startled cry.

'Who are you?' a woman asked. 'What are you doing here?' She had been asleep on the floor. In fact, she had been there all the time.

'It's all right, nothing to be afraid of,' Margulies said. He had no idea whether he was talking to a Jew or Gentile. She explained that she had climbed up into this little room, but had no idea where she was. 'I'm completely lost.'

The men explained that they were living together down in the sewers, where it was safe. She should join them.

'No,' she said. She had been down there since the liquidation, but couldn't take it any longer.

Margulies explained that she was no longer in the sewers, but in a cellar beneath the barrack. She peered at the light coming through the hole in the floor and declared that she wanted to get out of the city, into the countryside. The men explained how dangerous this would be, that there was little chance of her getting

83

through the town unnoticed, but she was adamant. They saw no point in arguing and so Margulies described for her how to get to the street, then to the Opera House and then the road that would lead out of town. They said goodbye to each other and watched her go. Then they slipped down the shaft, Berestycki clutching the stove.

Margulies became quite adept at these forays up into the barrack. As he seemed always to be away on brief expeditions to dangerous waters, returning laden with treasures, the group decided he had earned the nickname 'Korsarz'. In English, corsair or 'pirate'. 'Korsarz' soon discovered that there was another member of the group willing to take such risks. Klara was a very quiet, unassuming individual. She has always claimed, 'I think basically I was a coward. I don't think most people would admit such a thing, but it's true. I just wanted to live, so badly.' Despite her modesty, Klara threw herself into whatever work was necessary. 'Whether it was a man's job or a woman's, Klara took it on uncomplainingly.' Paulina reflected.

For Korsarz, Klara became a real companion, someone who was prepared to share responsibilities, and the risks. 'She was a real mover. She would do it, she would get up and go. One day, after I had been up a couple of times, I wanted to go back to the barrack, but Chaskiel was ill and preferred to stay behind. So Klara came with me. No one else would go ...' Margulies recalled.

They moved about the empty barrack together looking for something to take with them. Klara remembered her first impressions: 'It was so sad, just a deserted dump. All the very best things were already gone. We brought whatever we could. A bucket, a saucepan. Maybe a dress and some shoes. Something to wash our face and hands.'

Korsarz had found a tray and given it to Klara to load with plates and cups. Suddenly they heard the sounds of boots crunching across the ground outside. 'And I remember, I dropped the tray! And God Almighty, you never heard such a crash. I thought, that's it, we're all dead now.' They froze, waited and heard nothing. Perhaps whoever it was outside was also waiting for them to make another noise. Nothing happened, and when Margulies thought it was safe, they moved quietly back into Weiss's room and down into the sewers.

After a little more than a week in the chamber, as they lay there dehydrated and in agonies with diarrhoea, they were suddenly hushed by great liturgical sounds that came down from the church above.

'The feast of Corpus Christi,' recalled Chiger.

Though there wasn't a Catholic amongst them, they all knew the great religious days of the Roman Church as well as any priest. Like most Polish cities, Lvov moved to the rhythm of the great Christian holy days. They could all recall past occasions when they would have watched by the side of the road as the procession made its way through the town to church. There, the powerful singing would soon make the building resonate, as it did that day, right down to the foundations. While above ground, the narrow streets would carry the music great distances, into other neighbourhoods.

As they listened to the service, the bright young sound of the children's choir pierced the stone work. Chiger's seven-year-old daughter remembered the experience vividly. 'I could hear the children going to church. They were talking to their mothers. I remember a little girl asking her mother for some flowers. And I asked my mother, when can I have flowers, when will I see flowers again?'

Somehow, out of the depth of their despair, Paulina found some small crumb of comfort.

'Someday you'll have flowers, I promise you.'

Whenever Socha arrived he brought with him news and encouragement. It was unquestionably the high point of the day. He'd ask about the children and perhaps bring them something to cheer them up. Chiger, though always glad to see him, found these visits frustrating. As Weiss was the leader, he naturally assumed responsibility for distributing the food. Halina became his assistant, taking the food from him and passing it round. This invested her, along with Weiss, with immense authority. It was a situation which irritated some people, especially Chiger, who were of the opinion that Weiss and Halina never distributed the food fairly. Chiger claimed that Weiss's own friends always received their ration of bread first; his mother, the Weinbergs, the Orenbach brothers and Halina. The others had to wait and seemed to get short measures.

This perhaps innocent practice was the kind of little issue that eventually led to mistrust, and then to deep resentment. Chiger began to have serious doubts about this man Weiss. He continued to turn the same question over in his mind: 'It puzzled me, what prompted Weiss to abandon his wife and daughter? Yet he had brought with him a young girl, Halina, and some of his friends.' This thought had bothered Chiger from the very outset. Indeed, he seems to have been somewhat preoccupied with it for he returns to it in his memoir again and again. Though there never had been, nor did there develop, any romantic relationship between Weiss and young Halina, she did assume the role of his assistant with some relish. Perhaps an air of haughty authority in this strange young woman annoyed Chiger, a man used to being treated with greater respect. Whatever the reasons for his suspicions, there is no

86

doubt that they coloured his perception of Weiss as someone less than trustworthy. Coupled with the issue of the food, it created something of a gap between Weiss and his group of friends and the Chigers.

Chiger was also irritated by what he considered to be Weiss's fawning obsequiousness in Socha's presence. He would listen with growing annoyance as Weiss and his friends engaged Socha in small talk as the food was handed out. Talk that was sprinkled with flattery and praise which, Chiger was amazed to see, Socha accepted uncritically.

What lay behind Weiss's flattery, and indeed behind the entire problem of the relationship with the Chigers, was money – or rather the lack of it. While it was generally accepted that the women would not have to provide for their upkeep, it had gradually become apparent that some of the men had been less than honest about their liquidity. Most people were ignorant about each other's resources and from the beginning it had been agreed not to be too forthcoming with the sewer workers, either. This was sensible, for if Socha was never told how much money they had, nor how it was distributed, then he could never be tempted to favour one member of the group over another. Chiger had always been in tune with this idea. He had assumed, probably correctly, that their survival depended upon their solidarity, their ability to act and think as a single unit and so, in the interests of solidarity, he never betrayed the fact that Weiss actually didn't have any money at all. The money due to the sewer workers was simply made up each week as though it had come from the entire group, and handed across. Only Chiger knew that Weiss was penniless, and only Weiss knew that Chiger was making up more than half the entire total out of his own pocket.

It is possible to speculate that Weiss, and perhaps some of his companions, felt extremely vulnerable under these circumstances. But if he felt in any way indebted to Chiger, he made no show of it. In Chiger's account, Weiss did nothing to acknowledge the imbalance in their relationship. Yet Weiss must have felt some anxiety about his situation, as from all accounts he seemed to be obsessed with securing his guarantees with Socha. Chiger was convinced this explained the gushing blandishments heaped upon Socha during his visits. But then, once Socha and Wroblewski had left, Weiss and his companions sat huddled together, incommunicative, deep in dour conversation.

The relationship between the Chigers and Weiss eventually set in motion a whole series of awkward under-currents. Though he had been the leader of the project from the outset, and his position had been unassailable, Weiss had gradually come to realize that the real power within the group, the real authority, lay with Chiger. From the accounts that are available, there is no evidence that Chiger had ever shown any sign of wanting to wield his authority. 'How could we take charge? We had two children to take care of,' recalled Paulina.

Yet there is no mistaking the anxiety he had about the Weiss faction, which he described as a 'destructive element … rebelliously inclined and not suited to co-operation.' He also described how 'some of these individuals separated themselves into small groups and whispered and planned troublesome plots to their advantage.' He also overheard '… conversations, complaining about how they were paying large quantities of money and yet were obliged to tolerate the most wretched conditions imaginable.'

There are elements of paranoia both in Chiger's account and in Weiss's reported behaviour. Nevertheless, it is clear that Chiger was worried by these soundings. Given that he believed their survival depended on mutual reliance and trust, he saw the situation as a growing threat: 'No one could escape his or her responsibility to the group … but the group was not well balanced.' That kind of objectivity was in short supply. They were all, to a greater or lesser degree, still traumatized by the events that had led to and concluded with the liquidation of the Julag. All of them had seen horrors which would haunt them for the rest of their lives. They were living under a constant though diminishing fear of being discovered and they were all coping with anxieties about the people from whom they had been separated. All of this might easily have caused a group to sublimate their feelings by means of a series of trivial complaints. It was the Chigers who felt most isolated. They tended to sit on their own, with their children on their laps, trying to keep out of harm's way. Paulina was certain that 'We would never survive with Weiss in charge.' All their anxieties about the future became rooted in Weiss. They felt they were subject to his whims and that there was nothing they could do about it. But if they felt friendless, then Weiss probably felt the same.

However, most of the others were not concerned with any developing factions. They were distracted from worrying about the future or reliving the past by getting on with the day-to-day needs of their survival. Margulies understood this and was always looking for work to do. Berestycki, though tied to Weiss through loyalty, remained a moderating voice. They all seem to have decided to stay away from money matters and leave all that to Chiger.

Perhaps it's worth examining the question of money in more detail, if only to try to understand the arrangements and place the situation in some perspective. Chiger claimed in his memoir that Socha was paid 500 zloties a day for food and for their protection. Chiger is the only source for this information, but there is also no evidence to contradict it. So how much was 500 zloties? This is a difficult question to answer simply because the German occupation so enfeebled the Polish economy that making a direct comparison with other currencies is now impossible. Certainly by 1943, the Polish zloty was so devalued, even within Poland, that the economy had virtually deteriorated into a system of barter. For example, a cigarette was far more valuable than a twenty-zloty note, while meat and fresh vegetables were commodities that commanded the highest premium.

At the time, the average monthly wage was around 200 zloties. For a sewer worker it was probably around 150 per month. So it would appear that Socha and his companions received almost the equivalent of their monthly wage – every day. But even this was not such a considerable sum. It was also calculated by the German authorities that it cost nearly 400 zloties a month to feed a non-Jewish citizen. Clearly, the average monthly wage was wholly inadequate. It is also worth noting what the German authorities had decided should be the daily intake of calories in occupied Poland. Germans were allowed to consume 2613 calories per day, an Aryan Pole 669 (which is virtually starvation level) and Jews in ghettos and camps, just 180. (An intake of 1000 calories per day is a weight-reducing diet.)

Now, Socha was having to provide bread, potatoes, onions, sugar – whatever he could manage – for 21 people. We also know that a loaf of bread cost around 70 zloties in 1943. Based on all these figures, we might make a rough estimate that out of the 500 zloties Socha was given each day, he might have been spending perhaps as much as a half of that on food. Once the remainder was divided between himself, Wroblewski and Kowalow, they would have been making roughly the equivalent of a loaf of bread a day for their trouble.[9] Not insignificant, yet nor was it a fortune. According to Paulina, 'We payed Socha a lot of money. A lot of money. And it was worth every single penny.'

Socha's ostensible occupation each day was the regular maintenance of Lvov's sewers. Kowalow, the foreman, tended to supervise everything from the street. A small kerosine lamp was lit and lowered down the manhole. Attached to it was an angled mirror that reflected an image of the flame back up the manhole. The supervisor watched the colour of the tiny red flame he could see in the mirror. Should the colour of the flame turn blue, it indicated the presence of methane and that meant the sewers had to be evacuated. (Their methods haven't changed to this day.) Stefak Wroblewski would descend first and await the tool bags stuffed with bread and potatoes. On one occasion, just as Socha prepared to lower the second bag, he was interrupted by a German soldier, who had been watching the operation and was curious about the contents of the bags. Wroblewski, with his bag over his shoulder, stood at the bottom of the ladder awaiting the second. The moment he heard the German's voice, he quickly stepped out of sight, only to see the second bag plummet into the water that flowed between his legs. He snatched it up and waited while they dealt with the German. Kowalow said nothing. Under these circumstances, he left the talking to Socha, who complained bitterly that the soldier had startled him, causing him to lose his grip on his bag of cement, which was now lost in the waters below. The German gazed down into the gloom and might just have been able to make out the gas detector lamp and the quivering glint of sewer water. He shrugged and the incident was over.

Socha and Wroblewski's arrival was heralded by the sound

they made shuffling their way through the pipes. As Chiger recorded in his memoir 'We could hear them making their way through the mud and water for about half an hour before they arrived. With bags under their arms and the carbide lamp suspended from their teeth, they crawled for a kilometre through a "Forties" pipe, arriving breathless and exhausted.'

The city was criss-crossed with a network of concrete pipes that had been laid when the sewers were constructed. They were designated either 'Forties', 'Seventies' or 'Eighties', referring to their diameter. Forty centimetres was about sixteen inches, and an 'Eighty' is almost three feet. (I have crawled some ten metres through a 'Seventy' and have no wish to repeat the experience.)

Weiss took delivery of the bags while Socha and Wroblewski caught their breath. As Weiss and Halina distributed the food, the conversation was sprinkled with the usual praise of Socha's extraordinary courage, inventiveness, ingenuity. Chiger thought to himself: 'If it kept Socha sweet, why spoil the situation?'

But on this occasion, the conversation turned sour. A serious confrontation developed about conditions in the cavern. Socha claimed afterwards that he had sensed for some time the tensions that had been developing beneath the pleasantries. All the whisperings and complaints that had been aired in his absence were brought into the open. The discussion, encouraged by Weiss, became more and more heated until it suddenly erupted into a series of blunt remarks about the fact that he was being well paid and everyone should receive 'better service'. The Chigers sat in silence throughout the scene, too embarrassed to comment. Socha, having assumed or having been invested with authority, had become responsible for everything.

Socha's response surprised everyone. He was a mercurial character. For the most part he was cheerful and eager to please, but when slighted he could become furious. At first he was stunned. According to Chiger, once he'd realized he was under attack, he retaliated by lecturing the group on the realities of their situation. That they were alive and, for the present at least, safe. All of which had, until then, depended upon his willingness to help. Certainly the money was an incentive, but it could hardly really compensate for the risks he and his friends were taking.

'There are things you ask for, which I simply cannot provide,' Socha said. Chiger claimed that Socha also reminded them '… that his original agreement was with the Chiger family only and that everyone else had simply become attached.' However, Margulies, Berestycki and Weiss himself, all presumed to have their own special relationship with Socha. According to Chiger, Socha's ultimate message was 'about discipline', without which he saw no hope of success. Chiger seemed to see some link between Socha's deeply religious views and a belief that discipline in adversity was a fundamental principle.

Though Socha must have been bitterly disappointed by their attitude, he never threatened to betray them. Instead, as he listened to more and more complaints, he confessed that he was deeply disappointed and discouraged.

'In the face of all this, you argue!'

Though there was no talk of betrayal, he did hint at abandonment.

'Why should we return? You demand the impossible.'

Naturally everyone was frightened by these remarks, Chiger in particular. They seemed so out of character with the jolly, beaming moon-face they had come to know. Normally Socha's presence issued forth calm and hope, but his words were bitter and the man seemed close to tears. After he and Wroblewski had departed, there remained a deep sense of foreboding. He had succeeded in concentrating their minds wonderfully.

Small groups gathered in corners to conduct long examinations of the situation. A constant murmur of voices, interrupted by looks and glances. The little space was rent with tension, suspicion and fear. Weiss's leadership had succeeded in creating nothing but anxiety and distress. Socha's reaction to the group's dissent had made some reconsider the position, and now it was Weiss and his closest friends who began to feel isolated. He tried to reassert his authority through arguments, threats, and bullying.

Twelve feet below the street, choking on bad air, coping with gut-wrenching pains while trying to control their irregular bowel movements, the whispers of a few conspirators soon became, for Chiger, the threat of disaster. For Weiss and his confederates, the situation must have seemed desperate indeed. Whenever he approached the Chigers, he smiled and spoke with great deference. Yet the Chigers noticed that at every opportunity he ran his hands up and down the hems of their clothes, looking for where they had hidden their money. When Chiger discovered one of Weiss's friends going through their pockets, a state of open hostility developed between the two camps. Weiss perhaps never understood how to hold the group together, but one thing was clear: he was running out of options.

Chapter VII

It had become the routine to fetch fresh water first thing in the morning, before Socha and Wroblewski arrived. About two weeks after they'd settled into the cavern beneath the church, Margulies and Berestycki set out together, having decided to make the long journey to where Jacob had fitted the tap. They made their way back towards the Peltwa, down to the tunnel where the doctor and his group had settled.

As they stepped into the entrance to their tunnel, they found that the normal gentle flow of water had reduced to a faint trickle around their feet. At the same time, the most putrid smell seemed to linger within. Margulies stepped into the tunnel and held his torch aloft. The odour grew stronger and a horror slowly gripped him by the throat.

In the beam of his torch he found a wall of bodies, pressed together in a kind of human dam. An army of rats, feeding on the bloated corpses, scattered as the light splashed about. At his feet Margulies caught sight of children's toys and here and there, the glint of stainless steel and glass. Slowly, it all became clear. In amongst the wall of flesh were the remains of the doctor and the contents of his medical bag were strewn across the floor.

Margulies recalled how on that crazed night he and Klara had fought their way along the ledge and he had seen this group huddled together with the doctor. Margulies and Berestycki had come across them again during a visit back to the barracks and Socha had mentioned them from time to time. Whether he had ever delivered food to them, Margulies didn't know. He presumed not, for the evidence before him suggested that they had all found a different solution.

One by one the doctor had injected them with cyanide, before finally giving himself the same poison. Then, as each body had fallen lifelessly to the floor, it had created a small dam against the flow of water. The water had rolled the bodies against each other creating a steep wall, behind which the water built up until the tunnel had been all but stopped up. Margulies called back to Berestycki and led him to the scene. As Margulies described it, each sweep of the torch seemed to disturb a nest of rats. They returned to the group and, when Socha arrived, reported what they'd found. He was horrified. Margulies offered to show him the sight, but he refused to go.

'Just pull them away into the Peltwa, otherwise they will cause a flow-back.' But he would not go with them to help. He seemed appalled at the prospect. Together, Berestycki and Margulies wrenched each corpse free of its hold, sending it down the tunnel towards the Peltwa. Suddenly, they all came free and a wave of putrid water, limbs and torsoes flooded past, threatening to carry them all away. Once the cargo had emptied into the river it disappeared. It didn't seem an odd form of burial at all, indeed it seemed curiously dignified.

Margulies and Berestycki's news about the doctor's group increased their sense of isolation and forced them to consider the possibility that they might be completely alone. For some this

96

was not an unnerving thought. The smaller the numbers the greater the security. For others, the prospect was terrifying. While there had been the possibility of contact with other survivors – the occasional message passed back and forth – there seemed a way of retaining some grasp on the real world. But the thought of being utterly alone in the sewers meant that they had to survive with the resources they had to hand, both mental and physical. Socha's news from the outside world became even more vital. But on his next visit, he confirmed their worst fears.

'All the others we left behind, scattered about – all dead. All liquidated. They had to leave the tunnel to find food and were caught ...'

Socha's account is confirmed by a survivor who had lived with some sympathetic Catholics in one of the non-Jewish areas:

> Hundreds of Jews hid in the sewers. For many days they stayed in the tunnels where the sewage of the great town flowed. Many of them died. Many went mad. Only after fourteen days did the survivors emerge, driven out by hunger. They put out their heads. Their faces had been contorted into grimaces. Madness was in their eyes.[10]

It seems no one in the street suspected that there might still be others, bravely holding out.

Meanwhile, Socha had further news.

'There are still arrests going on, though not so many. Some Jews with forged Aryan papers were handed over to the authorities by some people ...'

'By Ukrainians?'

'Ukrainians, and Poles. They shot the Jews. The ghetto of course no longer exists and people go scavenging for whatever

97

they can find. You know, Jewish treasure.'

With Socha's news they were left with no choice: they had to stay in the sewers, somehow cope with the conditions and with only the faces they saw before them. The personalities, the strengths, the weaknesses, the tempers, the irritations, and the fears that had already begun to flourish in that tiny space were all they would know for months to come. Apart from their courage, all they were left with was the hard physical reality of their domain.

The everyday hardships they had to contend with both increased the stresses between them and at the same time focused their minds on survival. The sheer filth of their environment is hard to recapture. The walls of the cavern were constantly wet and crawled with a weird strain of albino insects. They were regularly invaded by small squadrons of rats, ferocious in their quest for food. These extraordinarily robust creatures scurried everywhere. If anyone tried to sleep, they were inevitably woken by a high-pitched clatter of cold feet across their hand or face. They appeared whenever the food arrived and fearlessly launched themselves at any unguarded scrap. It finally befell one of the group to stand guard with a pile of stones to throw at the beasts while others slept or tried to eat.

After a number of weeks some semblance of order had begun to evolve, the beginnings of a routine. Weiss maintained his role as leader, arbiter and ultimate authority and was still assisted by Halina, who had assumed an air of superiority amongst the women. The 'Princess', they called her, with her long tresses of hair which she combed obsessively.

Despite the rumblings from Weiss and his colleagues, there developed a spirit of hope. But then, quite without any warning, everything was thrown into confusion again. While the sewer workers were visiting one day, two young sisters stepped forward to speak with them. At first they spoke quietly and without rancour, but when their words were brushed aside they became angry. They could not cope with the conditions any longer. Nor could they tolerate not knowing how long their confinement had to last. They were adamant. Once the full measure of their feelings had been expressed, Socha and Wroblewski who had patiently listened, said nothing to try and discourage them. But their outburst came as a complete surprise to Weiss and Chiger, who had serious misgivings about letting them go.

Chiger interrupted to lecture them on the hopelessness of returning to the surface. He explained the realities of the liquidation and the consequences for any Jew discovered alive. Margulies pitched in and described what it was like up above, but their arguments only seemed to make the girls more desperate to leave. They pleaded, even begged to be shown out of their dungeon. Socha and Wroblewski suggested that it might be possible to find a Catholic family somewhere that might give them refuge. Paulina later recalled: 'They were both quite pretty, with good faces – not Jewish looking.'

Then someone spoke up. 'I'll go with them. I have some money. It might be possible to do something for the girls.' He suggested trying to contact some trustworthy Catholics, offering them money to take the girls in. 'Maybe we can find something outside.'

No one now recalls who he was, except that he had come from Turka, Halina's home town. His intervention was just what the girls needed and it was settled.

Margulies explained: 'If you go, you go late. After dark. The police and Gestapo will be waiting for you. They know there are Jews in the sewers.'

Socha described how they could get up to the street and then he and Wroblewski left. Later, the three of them were wished good luck and long life as they took their leave of each and every member of the group.

'Remember, no one can give you a contract to live,' Margulies said as they left. No one knew their names, nor anything else about them. It was only days later that Socha reported that the girls had been captured and shot. Nothing was ever heard of the man who left with them.

The news fell upon them like a shroud. Further proof, if any were needed, of the terror that still prevailed on the streets above. It can only have strengthened the feeling of being utterly trapped or imprisoned. Inevitably tension increased and tempers short-ened. Paulina recalled the rising tension: 'We remained an unhappy group. Unbalanced and at odds with each other.' She also commented on how Weiss's leadership continued to stir up resentment and fear. 'I wouldn't allow my children to wander away from us. I was afraid we would be separated.'

The atmosphere became highly charged and was likely to explode into arguments without warning. Perhaps a child had begun to cry – or had been crying for some time. Pawel was still in desperate pain, doubled over with fierce peristaltic cramps. He had never cried very loudly. He and Krisia had taught them-selves self-restraint while hiding in the ghetto. Kristina recalled: 'Because we were afraid of being discovered, we knew we always had to be quiet. We learnt to cry without making a sound, we swallowed our tears. It is still the same today. Whenever I'm cry-ing, nobody knows. It goes in, it doesn't go out.'

But then suddenly one of Weiss's colleagues rose to his feet, holding a pistol in his hand.

'Stop that crying. Shut up, or we will shoot you!'

Chiger froze with terror. Paulina took hold of her two children and held them to her. The eldest recalled the scene.

'If you cry, we will kill you. You cannot cry here.' The words became etched on Kristina's memory. Pawel had probably not understood; the rest of the group understood perfectly. Paulina did what she could to comfort her son, while Chiger said nothing for the moment, and waited for Socha's return.

The next day, as the sewer workers were preparing to leave, having delivered the food, Chiger slipped Socha the week's money. Rolled up inside was a brief note. It described the threat to Pawel's life and Chiger's fears about Weiss and his friends. As Socha departed there was a signal from Chiger that meant there was something for him inside the roll of money. An hour later, they heard the familiar grunts and shuffles of Socha and Wroblewski making their way back towards them down the narrow pipe. When they emerged the sewer workers immediately confronted Weiss.

'Hand over your weapons,' Socha demanded. Weiss was taken completely by surprise. He glanced across at Chiger and the others and moving very slowly, surrendered his pistol.

'Now listen very carefully. If any harm comes to the Chigers, we'll kill you. The only obligation I have is to protect these people,' he said waving his pistol at the Chigers. 'Everyone else is lucky to be here. Does everyone understand that?'

The sudden confrontation completely shattered any illusion that Weiss's flattery had purchased any goodwill with Socha. He was tactically and literally disarmed. Weiss got to his feet and made deep and profound apologies to everyone and claimed they had never intended to threaten Pawel's life. He swore that nothing like it would happen again. But in the silence that followed Socha's departure, the abyss yawned even wider.

It must have been clear to most of them that reconciliation could, at best, be only cosmetic. Fear and suspicion were now rampant. Margulies, Berestycki and most of the others tried to remain apart from the dispute, preferring to concentrate on the business of survival. But for Weiss, his situation was now virtually untenable. He found support from just four friends; the Orenbach brothers, Halina and Shulim Weinberg. Their whispers became more furtive, their conspiracies appeared more sinister. Chiger was convinced they were planning an attack on his family, destroying their security and endangering everyone. On the other hand, Weiss and Weinberg, being without money, were probably equally anxious that Chiger might simply refuse to support them any longer, assume the leadership of the group and banish those that could not pay their way. (One of the Orenbach brothers did have money, but he appears to have kept this from everyone.) Whichever way Weiss chose to look at it, the confrontation with Socha had unquestionably strengthened Chiger's position. From his perspective, it must have been the turning point. 'Now that they didn't have their guns, what could they do?' Paulina recalled.

Chiger clearly enjoyed Socha's support and perhaps under those circumstances Weiss imagined it was only a matter of time before Chiger tried to assert himself. But there were other elements to the equation. Weiss's mother was ill. She had been infested with lice before they had entered the sewers, was asthmatic and terribly weak. The cold, damp conditions only made her health worse. Weiss doubtless calculated that, if anything ever happened to him, the others would take care of a sick elderly woman.

Shulim Weinberg may have had similar thoughts. He and his wife shared a secret they had kept from everyone else. There wasn't

102

the slightest doubt in their minds that if it had been commonly known that Genia was pregnant, they would never have been selected to go with Socha. It's clear that Weinberg was deeply loyal to Weiss but in the light of the hostility between Chiger and Weiss's clique, he must have worried about how to protect Genia. For the Orenbach brothers, the problem was simply one of allegiancies and they had been committed to Weiss from the start. Very little is known about Itzek and Chaskiel, except that they were both in business and had come from the town of Radzyn.

In the atmosphere of growing uncertainty, Weiss and the three men closest to him decided to act. It is impossible to imagine that they came to their decision easily or without knowing the probable consequences. They had decided to leave the sewers and take their chances on the street. Under the greatest secrecy, they sought the opinions of others. According to Margulies, 'Weiss did not trust me. He wouldn't talk to me. Instead he spoke with Berestycki and asked him to ask me if I would go with them. I said no and Berestycki said no.' Jacob was plied and cajoled but with no success, and when it was clear he wouldn't leave, Chaskiel Orenbach changed his mind.

'Come on, we're all going to die anyway. They're dead already,' Weiss argued.

Chaskiel said no. He would stay. It seems Weiss had not intended to include Halina in his plans. She would be left, along with his mother, to get on with the rest of the group. Nothing was said to Chiger or Socha in case they tried to prevent their escape. Finally the day came. Their announcement came as a complete surprise to Chiger, but they argued that the conditions had got the better of them. According to Chiger, Weiss explained: 'The wild strawberries will be out and I want to taste them again.'

They planned to go down to the Peltwa and simply follow it to where it emerged above ground. Having calculated the risks, Shulim had decided his wife would be safer in the sewer, and said goodbye. What words passed between the two Orenbach brothers are gone forever and according to Chiger, Weiss did not speak to his mother at all. 'What could she do? When the men had gone, she and Halina were abandoned. Especially Halina. She sat there next to Mrs Weiss. It was so sad.'

When Socha heard the news he cursed the men who had fled. He knew they had no chance, and when they were captured, what then? Margulies understood the situation perfectly. No matter how resolved they were to keep silent, they would not last long.

'Once the Germans have you, you will talk. There's no question. They will beat you and torture you. Who could resist?'

Chapter VIII

In the days and weeks that followed Weiss's departure there was increased vigilance for any sign of intruders. Socha and Wroblewski took greater precautions entering the sewers, using a different manhole each day. 'Korsarz' Margulies and Chaskiel Orenbach continued to make quick forays up to the barrack to fetch more material: clothing, another kerosine stove, a bucket for making soup.

They also brought back reports of how the rest of the ghetto was being systematically stripped of every possible durable item that could be carried, pushed or thrown on to the back of a cart. Eiderdowns, beds, blankets, tables and chairs, everything. They watched as entire families carried out suitcases filled with loot, while Ukrainian police stood guard.

Meanwhile, Korsarz saw teams of labourers, probably from the Janowska camp, slowly demolishing the empty buildings with their bare hands. It was as though the ghetto was not only being stripped bare, but that all evidence of their existence was being expunged – and it was being carried out in the most callous fashion. There were no signs of any special activity, no evidence that the SS or Ukrainian militia were combing the buildings for anyone in hiding.

Perhaps Weiss's flight had gone completely unnoticed. Perhaps they had made it.

On that particular trip to the barrack, one of them absent-mindedly kicked a stone, which echoed across the empty room and caused a Ukrainian militiaman to stare across in their direction. 'Each time I came up, I said to myself, this is the last time. Never again,' declared Margulies. The guard caught sight of Orenbach and the two of them made straight for the entrance to the cellar. They got safely into the sewer system and were not pursued. Nevertheless, it was obvious that these expeditions would have to cease. Soon the place would be cleaned out and the building itself demolished.

On their next visit, they found that the slab in Weiss's floor had been fixed solid, probably by boards that had been nailed across it. To attempt to force their way through would have been suicidal. But Margulies, determined to maintain contact with the outside world, decided to find another way. He took the most obvious course, which was to follow the Peltwa down the chamber until it emerged at ground level. Margulies remembers it was still light when he emerged at about five in the evening. He stepped out into the world beyond the old ghetto boundary, but was immediately stopped in his tracks by what he saw before him. There, sprawled on the ground, no more than a few yards from the opening, were the bodies of Weiss, Shulim Weinberg and Itzek Orenbach. It appeared they had been shot the very moment they had emerged.

It was then more than five weeks since the liquidation and the sight of three Jews emerging from the sewers must have been a story the executioners told with some relish: 'Imagine being down in the sewers all that time!' It's possible that they linked the incident with the sighting of Chaskiel Orenbach in the barrack and perhaps even suspected that there were others still hidden somewhere in the labyrinthine tunnels. Socha was fairly well tuned to all the rumours and reported whatever he heard.

Margulies dragged each of the bodies to the river's edge and pushed them, one by one, into the current. Old Mrs Weiss was comforted by Paulina. Chaskiel Orenbach's reaction is not recalled, but, according to Chiger, Genia Weinberg took the news with a stony silence, but later wept quietly with Halina. A bond had developed between the young girl and this beautiful and tragic woman. She had already lost two children to the Nazis. All she had now was the memory of her third child, a daughter, whom she had given to Ukrainians to look after, and the secret baby that was still growing inside her.

There is a divergence between the separate accounts of the death of Weinberg. Mrs Weinberg's account claims that her husband met his death fetching water: 'Two men had gone for drinking water. One fell in and was pulled along by the current and never returned.'

However, Chiger's account, corroborated by Paulina, their daughter Kristina, Margulies and Klara, is clear Weinberg perished with Weiss at the mouth of the Peltwa, no more than five weeks into their ordeal.

When the news was broken to Socha he gave some intimation that he had already heard the news from another quarter. His only positive response was to inform Chiger, 'You are the leader now.' Halina, now abandoned, approached Chiger and asked if she might 'join his group', she wanted his protection. She confessed, 'All I have is one 20-zloty note. Nothing else ...'

There was no doubt about letting her stay, but her asking to 'join' seemed to indicate that the gap between Weiss and the others had been considerable. Chiger resolved that he would never

107

allow factions to develop. From his perspective, Weiss's departure had meant that the threat to his family was gone. It was sad that he was dead, but, 'We could never have survived with Weiss. It had been impossible.' Chiger was philosophical about the episode. He felt that it had a unifying effect on the group, committing them all to greater efforts towards their common welfare.

The tragedies that befell Weiss and his companions came at a time when the fifteen that had remained were finding their environment increasingly dangerous. The daily routine of collecting water was an exhausting and difficult exercise at the best of times. It was now fraught with danger, as the sewers had become underground cataracts. Late June and early July marked the season of the annual summer rains: wild electric storms, coupled with massive down-pours that quickly filled the gutters and the storm pipes under the streets. The rains completely transformed the sewers into chambers that thundered with the noise of the vast quantities of water that rushed towards the Peltwa. The river rose above its banks, flooding the ledges to a height of two feet.

Not only was the main chamber then impassable, but also travelling down any of the network of tunnels had become a treacherous exercise. 'Torrents of water would cascade through the pipes and we were in constant danger of being carried away,' wrote Chiger.

Once the Peltwa had become swamped, water flowed back in the opposite direction, creating a backlog of water, which eventually filled the system. Pipes that normally carried water away swiftly simply didn't work, the system was flooded and they became trapped, for up to twenty-four hours, unable to leave the cavern.

With each new storm, the waters in the system brought with them debris and silt from the streets above. This clogged up some of the tunnels they used each day, and it had to be cleared away. It was hard, back-breaking work, but it simply had to be done. One morning, Chiger and Berestycki returned from 'digging and clearing away the mud and slime at the end of our tunnel'. They collapsed exhausted from their labours and looked forward to a rest while they awaited Socha's arrival. Then Chiger realized it was his turn to fetch the water, but before he could get to his feet, Kuba was up and had volunteered to go in his place. His brother-in-law was a delightful character; he may not have been the most agile of men, but he had about him a distinguished air, an elegance which earned him great respect. Despite his cultivated manners, he never avoided rolling up his sleeves and pitching in with some of the most loathsome tasks.

'Go to Pepa. She is alone with the children and needs your company. I'll fetch the water,' he said.

Outside, the rain had begun to fall gently. As Kuba prepared to go, Margulies took Chiger to one side. 'I said to Chiger, "Don't send him,"' recalled Margulies. 'But Kuba used to feel guilty about not doing enough work and he would say, "It is my turn to fetch the water."'

Kuba and Orenbach set off together with the empty containers. While they were away, the rain turned into a shower and they could hear the waters begin to thunder through the pipes. Margulies continued, 'I would always give him a lecture, "if it rains, the tunnel will fill and it will lift you up and you will be carried forward – remember the floor is so slimy."'

Everyone knew the danger the two men were in, but there was nothing they could do.

'As the rains got worse, my father got more and more worried about Uncle Kuba. The pipes became filled with water,' Kristina recalled. Perhaps an hour later, they heard the sound of someone approaching. Chaskiel Orenbach emerged from the tunnel, alone.

'His face was long and sad. He slunk against the wall and it said everything that needed to be said. He wept and explained that Kuba was no longer with them,' Paulina remembered.

According to Chiger, Orenbach told them, 'While Kuba was filling his jug, a sudden fresh influx of water surged through the pipe they were in and carried him away.' Orenbach claimed that he too had fallen into the torrent and only managed to crawl out with great difficulty. He also claimed later that because he didn't have any dry clothes to change into he remained cold and damp for weeks. He saw this incident as the cause of his subsequent tuberculosis.

For the Chigers, Kuba's death was a tragic loss. Kristina was deeply fond of her uncle. Apart from the fact that Kuba Leinwand had been a tireless helper, especially in looking after the children, he had also been the last link with Chiger's sister. For years, Chiger reproached himself for not having refused Kuba's offer to fetch the water. His final word on the incident was of little comfort:

He had slipped into the Peltwa during the first minutes in the sewers. An hour or so later, he had fallen in and I had to drag him out with my belt. Now when he did not have to face the river again, he perished in the same waters – the waves of destiny.

It must have seemed at this time that they were stumbling from one catastrophe to another. After a journey through the flooded tunnels to fetch water one day, Chiger sat down and wrenched off his water-logged boots. Being made of felt, they willingly absorbed water and resisted all attempts to dry them out. He began massaging his swollen feet and, to his horror, discovered something missing. Before entering the sewers he had strapped a precious gem between his toes as a precaution against losing it. The gem, worth a great deal of money, had been a kind of insurance policy against the unexpected. Something that would have sustained their existence for months, if necessary. His feet had become so swollen and water-logged that the strapping had disintegrated and he'd lost everything when removing his boots. The lamp was brought over and they searched everywhere, but the gem was not found. Chiger concluded that it must have been lost on a previous occasion when he had been too tired to notice.

Feeling wretched and depressed, he took his cheap felt boots and a pair belonging to one of the children, and hung them out to dry. Immediately above their heads, in the centre of their little cavern, was a shaft that led up to a manhole. It had never seemed a threat before because Socha assured them no one would ever have any reason to enter the sewer from that point. At the top of the shaft, the manhole cover allowed in a faint chink of sunlight and a little dry air. Chiger hung the boots under the manhole cover where they had a better chance of drying out. They were left there throughout the night and into the next morning.

The men had just returned with the morning's supply of water and were waiting for Socha and Wroblewski, when the sky, quite literally, fell in on them. Without any warning there came the sound of heavy steel grating against concrete and a shaft of sunlight poured down from above. Someone had lifted the manhole cover. They froze. It was their worst possible nightmare. From above their heads they could hear voices. Polish voices, not German. Someone

111

was talking about investigating. He was speaking about having seen something through the grate of the cover and was now brandishing his discovery, a pair of felt boots. Margulies recalled that, though blinded by the daylight, 'We pushed the women and children into a corner and quickly made a plan.' No one dared make a sound. The light didn't spill far down the shaft, so they suspected they had not actually been seen. They waited.

'If they come down, we'll grab 'em and knock 'em down. Then dump them in the water – finish,' whispered Margulies.

Like a bad dream they heard the sound of someone descending the shaft, his heavy workman's boots clanging on to each step on the way down. As the intruder stepped into the little cavern, he was completely blind in the inky gloom. Margulies had picked up a shovel and waited. The intruder took out a match and lit it, but it offered him no help.

Margulies brought the shovel around with all his strength and clubbed the unsuspecting intruder across the back of the head. He let out a cry, of both terror and pain and immediately threw himself back up the ladder. He scrambled towards the street screaming at the top of his voice, while those down below gathered up everything they could possibly carry and began their flight. Margulies and Chiger shouted, 'Run, run!'

In the meantime, the intruder emerged into the street yelling, 'There are Jews in the sewers! There are Jews in the sewers!'

He ran to his colleagues to tell his story. It was true, just what everyone had suspected. Jews in the sewers. They'd all heard rumours, whispers, but this was proof. The simple Polish worker was prey to all the most ignorant fantasies about the Jew in his community. Among the most commonly held convictions was the belief that if you could discover the Jews' hiding place, there you will find their treasure. It had a naive quality not too dissimilar to the myth about Irish leprechauns. So it was the anticipation of jewels and gold that excited the men in the street, not any duty they might have had toward their Nazi occupiers to report their discovery.

Beneath them, the group had already begun to take flight. They felt they knew the sewers sufficiently well to put some distance between them and the cavern, and then they might have a good chance of not being discovered again. The fifteen stumbled along together, down treacherous paths and ledges still flooded with the summer rains. They turned into a tall elliptical tunnel that had a narrow trough, less than ten centimetres wide at the base. It slowed their progress, forcing them to walk along the trough placing one foot in front of the other. Chiger carried Krisia on his back, while Paulina bore Pawel. Suddenly she came to a halt. One of her wooden shoes had become wedged fast in the trough and would not budge. She lunged forward, twisted her ankle painfully and could not move. She called out to her husband for help, while Korsarz, ahead of everyone, urged them on.

Chiger turned round, 'Get up, Pepa, get up! We can't stop now ...!'

He tried to dislodge the shoe but it would not give. It and Pepa were stuck fast. In the distance they caught sight of a light. Some lanterns ahead. As they came closer they heard Socha's voice calling out to them. 'What are you doing here?' they asked him. He'd already heard the news from his colleagues in the street, he said, but hadn't expected them to be so far from the cavern. It had been another sewer worker who had discovered them. Apparently, he had returned with some of his colleagues but the place was already deserted. But from the evidence they saw all round them, stoves, pots and pans, there was no doubt any longer. Everyone knew there were Jews in the sewers.

'There's no point in going back there. We'll have to find somewhere else,' Socha explained. He already had somewhere in mind. But first Pepa had to be removed from her shoe. The shoe was unfastened, she was lifted on to Socha's back and then carried down the tunnel. Chiger finally wrenched the stubborn clog out of the trough and followed behind.

Socha led them down a difficult and confusing route and finally paused at the entrance to a Forty. They had to crawl through it to reach their next sanctuary. Each in turn was lifted up to the pipe and helped along the way. There is a simple rule understood by 'pot-holers' and sewer workers alike: if your head and shoulders will squeeze through, everything else will follow. Progress was good, until Genia Weinberg squeezed into the Forty. She had managed to get herself halfway in when suddenly she got stuck.

'Crawl, crawl forward!' they begged of her. She could not move. No one could understand it. Her coat was perhaps too thick and heavy.

She became frantic, not being able to move one way or the other. She knew the reason to be something far more substantial than an overcoat and was terrified in case the others discovered the truth. Finally, Margulies took hold of her legs and pushed her painfully through the pipe, just sixteen inches wide.

The place that they came to was described by Chiger as a sort of cave with rough-hewn walls and an uneven floor. It was somewhere within the foundations of a building but still very close to the surface. Once they were all inside, they realized that they could clearly hear conversations from the street. If they could hear what was being said above them, surely they would be audible at street level. Socha acknowledged that the location would not be suitable, and set off in search of somewhere else.

They had not spent one full night in the cave when he returned with news of yet another location. Another journey, through tunnels and pipes. By now, most of them were beginning to recognize certain landmarks and could vaguely discern their location in relation to the streets above. Somehow their spirits rose on this apparently endless search. Kristina remembers being carried on her father's back down to the main chamber where the Peltwa flowed:

Suddenly we came to a very large space. It seemed like an underground boulevard. It was light, bright and so, so big. I found it quite shocking, but I was so terribly happy that I started singing.

My father put me down, and while I was walking I trod on a hatpin. It went straight through my foot and although I was bleeding a lot and I must have been in pain, my spirits were so high I didn't seem to care about it. I bent down and pulled the pin out again and carried on.

Once they'd left the main chamber they seemed to be climbing higher, closer to the street. They came to a halt at a very difficult location, beneath a large manhole. They were at the junction of three large storm pipes that joined at the edge of a large shaft, right at their feet. This shaft went straight down to the level of the river, perhaps another metre and a half below, where it emptied. Above their heads was a large hinged cover which was opened during the winter so that snow from the streets could be swept straight into the sewers. In the side of this wide snow shaft, again above their heads, was the entrance to a chamber that Socha claimed 'would be dry and somewhere you could remain indefinitely'.

115

He helped the first man through, handed him the lamp and then one by one the rest followed. All of them climbed through but one, who had decided that was the moment to quit. It was another whose name has not been remembered. He told Socha he had had enough and wanted to return to the street. 'I have some Aryan friends who will give me shelter,' he claimed. He bade everyone farewell and Socha and Wroblewski led him out. He was never heard of again.

This, their fourth sanctuary in less than seven weeks, was easily the worst. The best that could be said for it was that it didn't flow with raw sewage. But it was not dry, in fact the walls were smooth with slime from a constant stream of water. There were two incoming storm pipes trickling water, which flowed out again through the pipe that had been used as an entrance. Through these pipes, a cold wind howled all night long. The ceiling was constantly wet and water dripped on to their heads. The penetrating cold and the renewed company of rats reduced their spirits to rock bottom.

They were still tired and in pain from the chase the night before, as well as being hungry and becoming soaked through. Paulina slept huddled over her children, allowing the constantly dripping water to fall on her back. When they stirred again in the morning, their muscles ached from the damp. They all agreed it was impossible. When the sewer workers arrived with the food, Chiger broke the news Socha was dreading to here.

'We had a dreadful night.'

'This place is impossible. We just can't stick it.'

'We must try and find somewhere we can stay for a long period of time.'

Socha conferred with Wroblewski and decided to talk it over with Kowalow. 'He knows the sewer system better than anyone.'

Kowalow thought about it and then agreed to show them somewhere worth looking at. They set out for the fifth time in search of somewhere to live. From the accounts that are currently available, the original group of twenty-one seems to have been whittled down to thirteen. Yet at this stage there is a contradiction, because the same accounts state that as they set out for their fifth hide-out, they were a 'family of eleven'. There is unanimity about the numbers originally selected to be sheltered by Socha, and about how many there were at this stage in the story. Yet no one can account for the loss of the other two; casualties of time and memory. So, as they set off, there was Ignacy Chiger, his wife Paulina, their daughter Kristina and son Pawel, Jacob Berestycki, 'Korsarz' Margulies, Klara Keler, Halina Wind, old Mrs Weiss, Chaskiel Orenbach and Genia Weinberg.

This time Socha took Krisia on his back, while Chiger carried Pawel. It was a shorter journey, to a spot very close to the cave-like place. They were led to the entrance. Chiger recorded in his memoir: 'It was very difficult to reach. It meant taking hold of a steel bar embedded in the wall and heaving up into a cascade of water coming from a Seventy.' They were then instructed to crawl through the pipe as far as it went. Chiger found the difficulty that presented itself somewhat reassuring: 'If we found it hard to reach, then so would someone trying to find us.'

The others looked at each other with great misgivings and hauled themselves into the pipe. They crawled along, allowing the flow of water to pass between their hands and knees. By comparison with other pipes they had known, the Seventy was quite spacious – nearly two foot six in diameter. At the other end they found themselves in a narrow room, about five meters long and about one and a half metres across. Adjacent to the pipe they had just crawled through was another compartment, again about five metres long, creating a kind of L-shaped room. In fact, what they had been brought to was called a storm basin or catch basin, usually constructed at the base of a hill to help regulate storm water.

Paulina came through with the children and immediately stepped across to the adjacent compartment and settled down on the floor. The men arrived and began to explore the place thoroughly. It was impossible to stand upright, which meant the ceiling must have been little more than a metre and a half high. In the wall immediately opposite the Seventy, about a metre from the ground, another pipe emptied rainwater from the street. This ran down the wall, across the floor and out the Seventy. To the right was an area filled with earth and rubble. The walls, built of closely masoned stone, were mouldy and covered in cobwebs.

Apart from the flow of rain water, the rest of the floor was dry. In fact, Paulina remembers that it was the only dry place she'd seen in the sewers.

The men got down to discussing the relative merits of the place. Some were for it, others against. Socha did his best to sell the place, because, quite simply, he was running out of alternatives. Seeing he wouldn't get a straight answer from the men, he came over to Paulina sitting on her own with Mrs Weiss and the children: 'He laughed and smiled at me. "What do you say Mrs Chiger?" I turned to him and I said, "Socha, it's a palace. It's a palace!"'

Chapter IX

'I have one more request, Mr Socha.' said Paulina.
'What is it?' replied Socha.
'Like you, I believe in God.'
'Yes?'
'I have always lit candles, even in the ghetto, even in the camp.'
'Candles?'
'On Friday I light candles, on Friday evening. Could you bring me candles so that I can light them at the beginning of the Sabbath?'

According to Paulina, 'Socha embraced me. He was very devout. He said, "I love believers. I'll bring you candles every week."'

At sunset on Fridays, or whenever she could judge it to be sunset, Paulina lit her candles, covered her eyes and whispered to herself, 'Blessed art thou, O Lord our God, King of the universe, who has sanctified us by thy commandments and commanded us to kindle the Sabbath light.' Every week, throughout the rest of their ordeal, Socha brought Paulina candles for Friday night.

The men returned to the room beneath the Church of Our Lady of the Snows and retrieved everything that had been left there. Stoves, jars of pickled cucumbers, barley, coffee, blankets, saucepans, buckets, cups and plates. With their shovels they scraped the walls and floor of their new sanctuary and did what they could to keep the place tidy.

A bucket was allocated for human waste, which someone dragged down the Seventy and emptied into the Peltwa each morning. Then they set off with a separate bucket to collect fresh water. They produced a basin for washing and each morning everyone washed their hands and faces and, once a week, stripped down and bathed completely. Socha brought them another lamp and with it a regular supply of carbide to fuel it. The lamp was suspended from the ceiling and blazed away, day or night. The old carbide lamp had been the standard form of illumination on most carriages and motor vehicles before the war. Carbide, a compound of carbon, when placed in a vessel with a little water, undergoes a chemical reaction which produces the gas acetylene. This is collected at the top of the vessel and fed to a small flame. The light produced from this flame, a soft yellow flare, was enough to see by and was relatively safe. Each morning the base of the tank was unscrewed and the used residue at the bottom dumped in the corner with all the rubble. Fresh carbide had been stockpiled in various locations throughout the sewers before the liquidation. When that ran out, Socha brought fresh supplies along with some kerosine for the stoves, and left it at some predetermined spot in the tunnels, where one of the men would go and collect it.

The business of collecting water also changed. Socha found another location that was closer, though far more difficult to get to. Despite the difficulty, the water supply was good and constant. They had to crawl down the Seventy and then into a Forty that travelled under the length of Serbska Street up to Rynek, the main square where the town hall stood. They then turned left down another Forty, which ran directly under the fountain of Neptune. Beneath the public fountain, where each day women queued with buckets and pitchers to collect the day's supply, water drained directly into the sewers.

Collecting the water was an exhausting and tedious exercise. It was usually carried out by two people and invariably one of these would be Klara. They would squeeze themselves into the Forty, one going backwards and the other forwards. The bucket was dragged, or pushed between them. According to Klara, 'You had to crawl on your stomach and manoeuvre with your elbows.'

They fashioned a special handle on the bucket which could be looped over someone's head, so they could drag the bucket with them. Having filled their bucket they would shuffle slowly back under Rynek, where above them Ukrainian peasant women stood selling bunches of dried herbs and wild flowers. They crawled under Serbska Street to the junction with Bernadinski Square, named after the monastery on its eastern side. There, in the street above, fresh green lawns sheltered by plum trees provided a welcome resting place for pedestrians. The storm basin where they were hidden was directly beneath Bernadinski Square.

Socha also helped to improve their sleeping arrangements. He knew the location of some timber which he claimed could be fashioned into beds. However, collecting the timber would involve a highly dangerous expedition, one which Korsarz revelled in. Socha took Margulies, Chiger and Berestycki on a long journey. Setting out to the west, they crawled beneath the square where stood the statue of the great Polish poet, Adam Miskievicz. There the pipe ran into an elliptical tunnel, in which they could walk upright a short distance to the Peltwa. They crossed the river at one of the little bridges and then followed a tunnel that ran under one of Lvov's great boulevards, Kopernica Street. At the far end of that, past a cinema and the main post office, they took a turn to the left, towards the Lonsky prison.

This infamous location had been used by the NKVD during the Soviet occupation between September 1939 and June 1941. When the Germans arrived they made great play of the appalling atrocities the Soviet secret police had carried out behind its walls. For the benefit of Nazi cameramen, Jewish labourers were filmed carrying out scores of corpses and stacking them up outside. During the Soviet occupation the corpses had been Ukrainian nationalists; under the Nazis, they were Jews and communists. Since the building had been commandeered by the Gestapo, it had been turned into a place of unqualified brutality and deprivation.

Way down in the foundations of the prison the Germans had constructed a bomb shelter, with an exit into the sewers. 'The bomb shelter had become flooded with sewer water,' according to Socha, '... [and so] it was abandoned.' The entrance to the bunker was a heavy steel door, in the centre of which was a large wheel that controlled a compression lock. 'We were standing right underneath Gestapo headquarters. We didn't know what we would find inside.' recalled Margulies.

Socha turned the wheel, heaved against the door and went in first. If he was discovered, he could at least claim to have some authority to be poking around in sections of the sewer. When he emerged again a little later, it was just as he said it would be – abandoned. Inside, the room was in some chaos. The floor was under several feet of water. There were stacks of shelves that had collapsed and a number of simple wooden bunk beds, partly submerged under mud and water. Everyday flotsam bobbed about on the oily black surface.

For Chiger, it was a treasure-trove. For Margulies, there was the particular thrill of plundering the very bowels of the Nazi police headquarters. There was far too much wood to carry out at once; they would have to make a number of trips. They lifted out some of the bunk beds, broke them down into smaller pieces, then made the long journey across the city to the Bernadinski Square.

The planking was filthy with mud and completely water-logged, but it was still invaluable. They decided to construct a large communal bed in the longer of the two compartments by wedging two or three beams crossways between the walls, then laying the planking lengthways up to the end. The waterlogged timber was initially very uncomfortable and probably unhealthy to sleep on, but it was either that or the floor. 'At least now we could stretch out properly for the first time. It made a big differ-ence,' wrote Chiger. 'We knew our body warmth would eventu-ally dry out the timber, which it did.' He went on to speculate: 'But did that mean that our bodies absorbed all the moisture? It was probably what happened, in which case terrible harm was done to our internal systems.'

During the daytime, the centre planks were removed, creating a galley between two opposite benches and, as the room was so low, they spent most of the time seated on these benches.

So gradually a daily routine emerged. They rose late in the morning and each took turns to wash in the water that had been left over from the day before. Berestycki would take out his tefil-lin, enwrap his arm with the leather thong, whisper the first verse of his devotions, then strap the little box against his forehead and intone the rest of the morning prayer. The carbide lamps were cleaned out and relit. The waste bucket was emptied and two people set off to fetch the day's water. On their return, perhaps an hour later, Paulina would take the oldest piece of bread and cut it into equal parts for everyone. She had assumed the role that had previously been Halina's.

Mrs Weinberg made coffee, sometimes sweetened with a little sugar, which they drank with their bread. The ersatz coffee, a mixture of chicory and cocoa solids, was stored in air-tight tins and replenished every two or three weeks. They never saw any milk, which, in any case, would have been impossible to keep fresh.

The bread too, would not last for long in the damp and musty atmosphere. The slightest morsel would attract the rats who made it impossible sometimes to eat a meal in peace. First, the bread was kept in a metal container with a lid held down by a stone. But the tenacious beasts still managed to get at it. Hiding the bread under the planks was tried, but this didn't work. Surrounding the bread with broken pieces of glass from bottles washed down into the sewer was ineffectual – the rats ignored the glass. Finally, the iron canister was suspended from the ceiling and this proved to be the solution. It also provided the children with hours of innocent entertainment, as they watched the rats going through the most exhaustive acrobatics, trying to reach the canister of bread.

They decided only to eat bread that was two or three days old, in case Socha was unable to make a delivery every day. This meant the bread was always mouldy. No matter, they simply cut away the white fungus on the crust and ate what was in the centre. After breakfast, they would sit together and talk, and wait for Socha. While they did this, they occupied their hands with the daily ritual of removing lice from their clothing. It was painstaking work, running their fingers up and down their clothes, and then plucking the lice, which they fed to the rats. Old Mrs Weiss had been lousy before they had entered the sewers, and now they were all infested. Paulina used to tend to 'Babsha', as they called the old woman. By now she had become quite somnolent, spending almost the whole day in her bed, her thoughts in some far distant place.

Then the familiar shuffles would announce Socha's arrival. The sight of his beaming face, illuminated by a row of shining teeth, became something of a symbol of his beneficence. 'He was like a guardian angel, just for me' recalled Kristina. 'Something sent from another world to keep me safe.' The fresh bread was placed in the canister and then he and Wroblewski would share coffee with them. Invariably Socha would share some of his lunch with the children. Kristina described their meals:

> He used to give my brother and me some of his cold pork sausage. I shall never forget the taste. It was so good, so tasty. He gave us each a small piece and I remember that I used to have a big piece of bread in one hand and the pork in the other. I'd try and make the meat last for a long time, so I'd take a big bite of bread and then a very, very small bite of the pork. It was so good.

In the meantime, everyone would gather round to hear the news. Rumours, gossip, fragments from the various underground movements: 'We were his captive audience. Huddled around him, eager for every morsel of news.' wrote Chiger. And Paulina recalled: 'Sometimes he used to stay for two hours, before going off to do an eight hour-day in the sewers.'

Socha also used to bring copies of *Das Reich*, one of the few newspapers that was published in abundance. Despite the distorted reports of the progress of the war, the Nazi rag was still devoured from cover to cover. Chiger used to take a macabre interest in the words of one of its columnists, Werner Lojewski, who wrote with almost hysterical superlatives about German victories in the east and, in particular, against the evils of the so-called 'Jewish conspiracy'. It must have seemed curiously unsettling to be reading this material, while hiding just beneath the conquerors' feet. Sometimes they also received copies of the *Polish People's Army* which, hardly surprisingly, contradicted *Das Reich* in all respects except the publication date.

Around midday they sat down to a lunch which, like the evening meal, usually consisted of soup. Genia Weinberg had taken on the responsibility for cooking. Her speciality was a potato soup. She began by frying onions, if she had any, then adding potatoes and water and boiling the mixture until the potatoes could be pulped. The soup was often enhanced with lentils or barley, which Socha seemed able to get fairly easily.

Chaskiel Orenbach loved the potato soup and taught everyone how to turn it into two separate courses. First by drinking the liquor – the 'soup' – and then by mashing the potatoes and whatever happened to be in with them – 'the main course'.

The purchase of regular supplies of food posed a number of problems for Socha. 'We were worried in case he got caught buying so much food,' explained Klara. 'We told him to buy it from different shops in different neighbourhoods, so as not to arouse suspicion.' But running about from shop to shop was something he had little time for. He had to employ someone else, and the most likely candidate was his wife Wanda. But letting Wanda into his secret posed a problem. Wanda, though 'an active and energetic woman', was temperamentally completely different to Socha. Like the majority of working-class Poles, Wanda had no sympathy for Jews. 'Go to your Jews,' she used to say to Leopold when out of patience with her husband, after being included in the secret. Socha explained, 'I told her not to breathe a word to anyone about what she knew. She doesn't know where you're hidden so you're safe. Besides it will do her no good to tell anyone. If the Germans ever hear that we are sheltering Jews, she will hang too.'

Despite her instinctive reluctance, she took up her new responsibilities with such enthusiasm that she even went so far as to buy a small peddler's pushcart, which she set up in the town square. If she was going to be buying so much produce, she might as well get it wholesale and try to make a profit. But she had further obligations. On Fridays, Socha collected the group's dirty laundry and brought it home for Wanda to boil and dry over the weekend.

*   *   *

After their lunch, everyone in the storm basin found something to occupy them during the afternoon, until they were summoned together again for the evening meal. After dinner there was further conversation and philosophizing. They would return to the newspapers, for any scrap of news that had been missed earlier and invariably find something worth arguing about. Chiger, in particular was especially interested in the political and military developments that were being played out above their heads. He discovered a willing and stimulating sparring partner in Halina Wind, who devoured the papers almost as avidly as Chiger, and her opinions were equally well informed. Halina had had the benefit of a good education. Her father had been a rabbi in Turka, where she had been brought up in an educated, perhaps even intellectual home.

127

They were the only ones who had finished high school. In fact, Chiger had attended the Lvov university. He'd attracted some notoriety in his youth because he had enrolled to study medicine in an institution that barred Jews from that faculty. In the event, he graduated with a master's degree in history and went to work for the Ministry of Sport where he became something of a local celebrity. Halina was equally proud of her own education. The two of them often caused the others to laugh amongst themselves, as they argued over who had had the better education, read the most books, or had a better understanding of politics … The men found Halina and her opinions constantly amusing. The women less so.

For most of the group, intellectual pursuits seemed at times a little frivolous. Margulies's notion was 'activity, constant activity' as the solution to anxiety. He had not ceased his forays up to the street. Indeed, he had become even more bold. As the ghetto area had been virtually demolished, except for some half-dozen workers' cottages that still remain today, there was no profit in trying to explore that area. Always waiting until nightfall before emerging, Margulies found safe exits in and around the area in which they were situated. During September he sometimes managed to climb the walls of the monastery and steal apples from the orchard. During one of these midnight rambles, Margulies was stopped by some Ukrainian militia.

'What are you doing here?' they demanded.

'I was hiding in the bombed out buildings.'

There were two of them, both with rifles. Margulies had slipped his pistol into his boot, but to get to it he had to lift the leg of his trousers. He was certain he would be shot on the spot before he got anywhere near his gun.

'Do you have any money?'

'I don't have nothing.'

Then a third militiaman arrived and declared that Margulies would have to be taken to the Commissariat.

'Why? What would you get, medals? Do you want medals?' asked Margulies.

Then a fourth militiaman arrived, this time carrying a powerful torch which he shone straight into Margulies's face. Margulies now couldn't see anything at all. The man looked at him and spoke in Ukrainian.

'Let him go. I know him well.'

Margulies didn't recognize the voice and had no idea who the man was. When he took away the torch, the four men were striding off in the opposite direction.

'I have no idea who he was. I never saw his face,' Margulies reflected.

In the dead of night, Margulies walked across the city towards some of the factories that had employed Jews before the liquidation. He had had some friends there once. He found the caretaker and chatted with him casually. Margulies felt that this was someone he could trust. He learnt that the factory still employed Jews who were marched every morning as a 'brigade' from the Janowska camp and at the end of the day's work were marched back again.

Chapter X

During September, the war against Germany took a number of dramatic turns. On Italy's Mediterranean shores, 1400 kilometres south-west of Lvov, British and Canadian troops had landed at Reggio and had begun the Italian Campaign. Five days later, on 8 September, the Italian armed forces surrendered. On 9 September, American forces landed at Solerno, German troops occupied Rome and Hitler announced his commitment to the defence of Italian fascism. As German forces in Italy came under growing strain, their commanders' reports in the east seemed sprinkled with the same word: retreat, retreat.

The Soviet summer offensive had generated a powerful momentum. Soviet armies recaptured Kharkov 800 kilometres east of Lvov, and the entire Donetz Basin down to the shores of the Sea of Azov. By 25 September, the city of Smolensk, 400 kilometres south-west of Moscow, was recaptured, as was Bryansk another 200 kilometres to the south. In the same offensive, launched from deep within the Russian heartland, Soviet troops seemed to be racing towards the great city of Kiev, capital of the Ukraine. The tide seemed to have turned. Some fragments of these events reached the eleven in the storm basin, and it seemed that once Kiev had fallen, liberation would soon follow.

Margulies had not given up on his expeditions to the street. As news of Soviet victories filtered down to them via Socha, he seemed to take greater risks than before. Not long after the encounter with the Ukrainian militia, he and Chaskiel had slipped out to see what was left to plunder from the old Julag. It was not yet nightfall and a brigade of labourers from the Janowska camp was still hard at work. The entire district had been reduced to rubble. Scattered over a field of shattered masonry, thin relics stooped over heavy stones which they lifted or dragged across the ground to the meaningless piles that had been designated at various points. Margulies looked out across the scene and knew there was nothing left here. But he was not ready to give up the search elsewhere. There might be something worth taking in some of the buildings nearby.

Tens of thousands of the men of Lvov had been sent to Germany to take up obligatory work service. Their wives laboured during the day in local factories, which meant that many homes were left unoccupied. Watched by Ukrainian guards from a distance, Margulies and Chaskiel moved through the field of labourers to the buildings along the perimeter. They slipped inside and moved quietly down the empty corridors, testing the doors as they went. They managed to slip into one or two empty rooms and emerged with a few bottles of liquor.

By the time they were in the street again, the scene had changed. They climbed to the brow of a small heap of rubble while behind them a group of noisy children played 'knuckles' in a crater at the foot of the hill. All across the open space, men were abandoning their loads and slowly shuffling towards the foreman, in preparation for the march back up the Janowska Road. Margulies and Chaskiel watched the brigade being counted and realized they were in danger of being the only figures left on the landscape. If they didn't get across the field of rubble quickly, they would be obvious targets. They began to crunch their way towards the brigade, now some way off in the distance. Suddenly they were stopped by a Ukrainian voice.

'Hella, hella, hella!' A militiaman was bearing down on them. 'Where are you going?'

'There – to join the group, the demolition group – lifting stones. We have to go back to the camp …'

'You're late!' the Ukrainian informed them.

'Well, you know we don't have a watch – of course we're late,' replied Margulies.

He had hoped to humour the militiaman, and for a moment it worked. The man turned and began to walk away. Then suddenly he rounded on them and this time he would not be so easily discouraged.

'Maybe you are partisans.' He had decided to make an arrest. Margulies reached down into his pocket and removed one of the bottles of liquor they had just stolen.

'Oh, so now you're trying to bribe me.'

Chaskiel had been watching Margulies the whole while, and had removed a short piece of wood that he carried as a club. The Ukrainian had no warning. Chaskiel swung the club into the man's throat and sent him reeling backwards. Margulies, meanwhile, had removed a hammer he had carried with him from the sewer. As the wounded militiaman staggered under the first blow, Margulies swung the hammer into the back of his head and brought the man down. 'He had no chance to live, not with a blow like that,' Margulies claimed afterwards.

He had fallen into some tall grass that hid him from view. Margulies and Chaskiel stood over the body ready to strike again, waiting. Over the hill of rubble the sound of children playing continued uninterrupted. The hammer was slipped back into Margulies's pocket and the two of them moved away from the spot. They began running and, though no one had seen the militiaman fall, some bystanders had begun to point at the two men. Margulies had got some way ahead of Chaskiel when he heard his friend cry out. He looked around and saw him struggling in the grip of some people who had decided to give chase. Margulies had no idea whether the dead man had been discovered, perhaps Chaskiel had just been unlucky. The children had abandoned their game and had gathered round, watching with mute glee, as if the Jew were some animal to be played with. Margulies had to help him: 'It was getting late, he was about to be handed over to the Gestapo. He would have been shot on the spot.'

Margulies took off towards the brigade and ran up to the foreman, whom he described: 'He was a capo – a good capo. He came from Catowice and spoke German.' Although the Germans still employed the Jewish police inside the Janowska camp, Margulies had no way of knowing whether to trust him. He just took a chance and described what had happened.

'Listen, try and save him. Go to those people and tell them he is one of yours.'

The capo agreed but Margulies held him back a moment.

'Hit him!' Margulies said.

'What?'

'Hit him – hard! ...'

The capo understood. He still wore the peaked cap and black armband which had invested the Jewish police with such awesome authority in the past. He confronted poor Chaskiel, who was stumbling under the grip of the crowd, and launched into him with a tirade of abuse. Then he leaned back and hit Chaskiel as hard as he could. The crowd was quite stunned by the capo's ruthlessness. He bawled at Chaskiel: 'Where have you been, you … you …? Were you lost? What happened to you?'

The crowd loosened their grip and Chaskiel fell to the ground. 'It's all right, he comes with us …' The capo hauled him to his feet and marched Chaskiel, stumbling across the rubble, towards the brigade. Chaskiel found himself thrown into the centre of the phalanx where he was surrounded by nameless faces who shuffled close beside him at the capo's orders. While all eyes had been upon the struggle over Chaskiel, Margulies had slipped away from the open landscape towards a safe building on the far side. From there he watched Chaskiel, barely sensible, marching with the others towards the Janowska Road.

When Margulies had returned to the storm basin, he recounted what had happened to their colleague: 'He's safe. He can look after himself. When they march back tomorrow, I will go fetch him.'

The others could scarcely believe Korsarz's account and they were less confident that they would see Chaskiel again. But the following evening, Margulies slipped back up to the street and made his way to the field of rubble. There he saw Orenbach, toiling away over the stones. Margulies signalled to him to edge his way towards the perimeter. Chaskiel did what he was told, while the Ukrainian police looked on. After another signal from Margulies, Chaskiel dropped his load and moved quickly out of sight. Margulies joined him behind a mound of rubble, where they waited for nightfall.

Back in the storm basin, Chaskiel could say little about his experience. He had been looked after by the men in the brigade and given food and water. He had seen one or two familiar faces behind the wire, but could think of no names. He was still shocked by whatever he had seen.

At one point in his account, Chiger described a romance that had developed and begun to flourish between Korsarz and Klara. Socha also would pass comment, confidently predicting that a marriage would come of the attachment. None had realized that the relationship had begun months ago, during the last few days before the liquidation. They also had no idea of the depth of feeling that had developed inside the hardy black-marketeer. Klara had always been the quiet one of the group. Prepared to get her head down and work her way through the ordeal, rather than become absorbed in the group's arguments. But that wasn't to say that she had no time for her own thoughts. The problem was that she had too much time. Over and over she remembered the scene in Weiss's room between Manya and herself before they were parted.

> I didn't know what to do. I felt selfish, because I had run away and left her. But I knew for sure that if I'd stayed with her I'd be dead. I just didn't believe any of those stories they were saying about us all going to have a good life ... I knew it wasn't true at the time. Only it was all at the last moment, the Germans were throwing people on to the lorries, so ...

Margulies would listen to Klara talk about Manya, wondering what had happened to her. There seemed no way of dispelling her guilt. She would constantly reflect on her parting with her sister: That was the most difficult thing I ever did. I was so upset about it because I left her behind and she could have been alive today. He was pulling me one way and she was pulling another ... I had no choice. To die with her or try to live.'

135

Margulies was not the sort of person to sit down with Klara and try and talk her through it. He had no words that might have made things any easier. Instead, he decided to do something. The idea had been formulating inside him for some time and Chaskiel's recent experience seemed to remove any doubts. He told Klara he would discover what had happened to Manya. According to Klara: 'So one day, he decided to go out. I had no idea how he was going to do it, because Jews were non-existent up there. The ghetto was gone, everyone was in the Janowska camp. Anyway he went out, and I thought, that's it – we will never see him again.'

Margulies made his way through the tunnels towards the Peltwa. Then he followed the river north, back towards the ghetto district. Along the way the river flowed under another of the great boulevards, Legionov Street, towards the Opera House. This magnificent theatre was built in the early nineteenth century, beside the River Peltwa. Along the banks of the river, a parade of trees and gardens were planted, leading up to the forecourt. There, its classic portico towers above the street. On the roof, a pair of gilded phoenixes stand on either side of a magnificent gilded goddess, holding aloft a laurel.

When the Peltwa was diverted underground it was made to run directly underneath the Opera House and, in the bowels of that stately palace, is a maze of tunnels that lead down to the river. Socha had pointed them out to Margulies on one of their sojourns together. Having found the right tunnel, he would emerge into a workmen's access chamber, built into the side of the building. From there it was simply a case of pushing open a pair of steel trap doors and stepping out into the street.

He waited until past midnight before emerging from the side of the building. The blackout gave him sufficient cover to cross

136

the wide open square to the safety of the narrow streets that led away to the west. He made his way to the factory where he knew the caretaker. He made contact and the caretaker led him inside the building and hid him in the rafters, above the shop floor. He planned to stay there until dawn, to wait for the workers from the camp, but he was discovered long before they arrived. A Yorkshire terrier that belonged to the works' foreman began circling beneath him, yapping and declaring his presence. The foreman came to investigate and pointed at him. 'Come down, come down now,' he shouted.

Margulies did as he was told.

'What are you doing here?' asked the foreman.

'Let me stay here tonight. I have to get back to the Janowska camp.'

Korsarz explained that he had been left behind when the brigade left the day before and he was waiting for the next shift. The foreman believed him. At dawn the brigade arrived, the men spread out across the shop floor and got down to work. They were producing cheap wooden furniture; stools, chairs and tables. Margulies moved unnoticed on to the shop floor and mingled with the workers, just another anonymous face. Apart from Klara's sister, Margulies also wondered about two of his brothers who had been sent to the camp some months before the liquidation. It was an attempt to make contact with everyone who could not be accounted for. 'I met this fellow,' Margulies recalled. 'He was from another town, and I said to him, give me your armband and stay here in the factory tonight. Let me go to the camp in your place.'

Margulies explained that he needed to make contact with people there and that he would return with the next morning shift. The switch was agreed. At the end of the day, the workers poured out of the factory building and assembled into two blocks of fifty, ten rows of five. In the heart of the group was Margulies wearing the armband. Each worker also had, embroidered on to his shirt just above the heart, his camp number, which, of course, Margulies did not have.

They marched down the Janowska Road, past a high concrete wall. The size of the complex was hard to gauge from the outside. It was not nearly as large as Auschwitz or Buchenwald, but it was substantial. Beside them, as they marched, were the tram tracks that ran from the heart of the city and terminated near the entrance. Along these they had efficiently transported thousands of people from the ghetto in the little open tram waggons. On the right, looming up before them was a large imposing gate, constructed in the Nazi neo-classical style: two massive, rectangular concrete columns supporting a plain concrete roof, and atop each column stood the German eagle and swastika. On one column was displayed the words: ZWANGSABEITS-LAGER DER SS (Forced Labour Camp of the SS). Straddling the road, beside the gate were two guard houses. It was at that point the road crossed the Lvov–Tarnopol/Kiev railway line and everything that lay beyond it was forbidden. As they marched past the guard houses and turned into the gate a guard barked at them:

'Kabben ab!'

Obediently, they doffed their caps and turned to the sentry who was counting heads. Margulies knew this was only a formality: 'All he wants to know is, are there fifty heads in each brigade? He doesn't look at your number. If he's got fifty, he's happy.'

They were marched down past some office buildings towards an inner compound, passing two sentry posts armed with machine-guns. Further on to the right, was a row of smart summer houses, to the left, a large compound surrounded by barbed wire. There, above the entrance to the inner compound, was the sign that had appeared throughout Europe wherever these establishments had flourished: ARBEIT MACHT FREI. They were led on to this parade ground, where they formed into ranks again to be re-counted. Margulies was standing right in the heart of the Janowska camp.

Though the camp had been there for less than two years, it was estimated that as many as 200,000 people had perished behind its walls. Pre-eminent throughout eastern Europe, its history was similar to that of a dozen other places. Soon after the Nazis arrived in Lvov they set about establishing their authority with well-rehearsed ruthlessness. Along with the sign posts in German, the proclamations announcing new laws and regulations, came the preparations to construct a forced-labour camp. The site was chosen by virtue of the location of the Janowska cemetery. The western half of the cemetery had been Jewish, which the conquerors had decided to flatten immediately under tank treads. On the ground that they cleared, some 150 metres away from the road, they constructed a relatively simply compound, surrounded by electrified wire fencing. Behind it rose a steep hill, at the foot of which there had been at one time a sand quarry, commonly known ever since as Piatski, or the 'sands'.

Around the parade or assembly grounds, they had constructed simple barracks to house the workforce. The capacity was doubled with the construction of a second series of barracks behind the first. At the southern end of the ground they built the workshop complex. This was a series of buildings where men laboured to produce anything from metal buttons for uniforms to leather belts, electrical fuses to door handles. It was a labour-intensive, all-purpose factory. The entire compound was completed by the beginning of October 1941.

It was not the only labour camp in the area. Within the vicinity of Lvov there were several labour camps, Kurowice, Jaktorow, Winniczki, Wielkie, Mosty, Brzuchowice, Dornfeld, Hermanow, and there were others. What singled out Janowska was its link with another camp, constructed and maintained in great secrecy – Belzec.

In 1940, the Germans constructed a labour camp near the village of Belzec on what had been the Partition Line that divided German and Russian occupied Poland. Quickly following the German attack against the Soviet Union in June 1941 work began on the expansion and transformation of the Belzec camp. During the winter months of 1941–2, the first gas chambers were installed and by March 1942 they received the first shipment, 1001 inhabitants of the town of Theresienstadt.

It was the first purpose-built death camp in Europe and was able to dispose of some 5000 people a day. The location of Belzec had been carefully considered. It lay some seventy-five kilometres up the railway line from Lvov to Lubin. South and to the east of Lvov, well served by good rail links, was the vast hinterland of Galicia and beyond it the Ukraine. To the west, again on a good line that ran across to Vienna, were Cracow and the major towns of southern Poland. Most of the transports to Belzec passed through Lvov, that is to say, through the Janowska camp, and the labour that was available there was exploited in the transportation process. Belzec did not have a large workforce, so much of the processing of those sent there was carried out by the workforce at the Janowska camp. After the trains had pulled in at the marshalling yards, the passengers were marched into the camp and on to the assembly ground. There, they were ordered to strip before they were marched back, naked, to the same transports. These trains, fifty to sixty waggons apiece,

140

would then complete the journey to Belzec, while workers at Janowska would sort out the clothing and other belongings piled on the parade ground.

The camp had originally meant to provide slave labour for the establishments inside the walls. As the complex grew, it provided labour to other factories in and around the city. This labour force was fed barely enough to keep it alive and was worked hard enough to ensure premature death. By February 1942, most people in the area had heard the name Janowska Lager and knew that being sent there was virtually a death sentence. Life-expectancy was only a few months. If the person was not beaten senseless by the guards, he would probably be starved on the derisory food, or engulfed in one of the epidemics that regularly swept through the barracks. The strong and quick-witted might survive six months. Because the death toll was so high, the population was constantly made up from the ghetto, hundreds or a thousand each time. What began as a labour camp had become an extermination camp. It was estimated that at one point the death toll had reached more than 2000 a week. Keeping up those numbers meant a constant supply of fresh labour, which came from all across Galicia and even from western Europe. Each morning brigades of men would shuffle out of the gate and march down to the various factories, like the Heereskraftwagen-park 547 (military auto-repair depot), and back again after a twelve- or fourteen-hour shift. The purpose was to use the human resource to the greatest possible economic advantage.

To cope with the growing population, the camp quickly expanded. Further up the road, at number 122, a site previously owned by a Jewish industrialist was taken over and there the SS established two industrial complexes: the Deutsche Ausreustung-swerke or DAW (German Armaments Works) and the Vereinigte

Industrie Betreib – VIB (United Industrial Plant). The entire complex now stretched down to the Janowska Road and along it for more than half a kilometre. A large concrete wall was thrown up around the DAW and VIB sites, which ran along the road up to the main gate. Beyond that was a twelve-foot-high brick wall, crowned with barbed wire which was overlooked every fifty metres by a watchtower. Behind the brick wall they constructed facilities to cater for a much larger establishment of officers and men that would run the complex. There were shops, a casino where the SS could be entertained with films and travelling cabarets, and even stabling for their horses.

On the far side of the inner compound was a row of villas that had been built before the war and which had been commandeered for the SS officers. SS Obersturmführer Gustav Wilhaus's villa stood towards the southern end of the row and afforded from its balcony a view over the entire ground.

Connected to the stables and surrounded by another brick wall, were the women's barracks. This prison within a prison stood at one corner of the main inner compound, but all links with the male inhabitants were limited by a double fence of barbed wire. It had been built to house up to 10,000 labourers, but in practice the working population rarely rose above 6000.

Margulies stood silently while his brigade was counted again before they could be dismissed. From within his brigade he had already met two brothers named Sukakhan, whom he felt he could trust. He had explained, 'I've come to search for somebody. A friend, a brother and sister perhaps ...'

Once the counting had finished, there was a mad scramble to the barracks to retrieve their kettles, in order to be fed. Margulies was given a spare one and then led to the kitchen. By the entrance, five-day-old cadavers were suspended from a gallows. They had been trussed up by the feet and then lowered into a large bath of water. Inside he was given a ladle of warm dirty water and a thin piece of dark bread. There he listened to the men around him describe the place where he now was.

Death had been established from the outset as the one and only form of punishment and when it was so easily and cheaply exploited, it became the norm, not the exception. Death was at the heart of every activity – and it sent men insane. Wilhaus, by all accounts, was a homicidal madman. Sometimes, if a new transport arrived carrying women and children, he had them brought up to his villa and, as he had no use for the children, had them thrown into the air while he took aim and shot at them from the verandah. He often did this in the presence of his little daughter who used to applaud his successes.

On other occasions he used to take aim at a labour squad on the parade ground, trying to remove a nose or an ear or a finger. After this, he would move amongst the prisoners to extract the wounded. He would then march them to the other end of the parade ground and finish them himself with a bullet in the skull.

Executions were stunningly macabre. Men were hung by the legs, beaten until dead and then sometimes even disembowelled. Everywhere was a kind of mad hatred, a violence that beggared the imagination. As the temperature regularly dropped well below freezing during winter, people were often simply left outside to freeze, or placed in large barrels of water. In the morning they would appear like elongated balls of snow on the ground, or their cadavers were chipped out of frozen barrels of ice. Untersturm-führer Fritz Gebauer, Wilhaus's subordinate was known simply to take hold of a man and strangle him with his own hands.

By 1943 the regime was confronted by different priorities. As

143

the Soviet successes had continued throughout the summer, the Germans began to find methods of disguising their work. They decided to remove any evidence of mass slaughter and the only way to do that was to dig up all the mass graves that were scattered throughout eastern Europe and dispose of the corpses. Colonel Paul Blobel, a former Einsatzkommando chief, was given the task of supervising this massive operation. Two weeks after the liquidation of the ghetto in Lvov, one of Blobel's units arrived at the Janowska camp. Out of the workforce they created new brigades, so-called 'Death Brigades', to dig up the innumerable mass graves scattered about the Piatski, and elsewhere.

Each day the Death Brigades marched to the sands where they shovelled tons of soil out of long graves, then climbed down into the pits and removed the decaying remains. In the process they retrieved any gold rings and the gold fillings from teeth. It was claimed by one survivor that 'each day we collected eight kilos of gold'. Meanwhile, a pyre was built out of massive logs and the putrefying bodies were then heaped on to the flames, which were fuelled by jets of heating oil, and consumed up to 800 corpses at a time. The same survivor recalled the scene:

> The fire crackles and sizzles. Some of the bodies in the fire have their hands extended. It looks as if they are pleading to be taken out. Many bodies are lying around with open mouths. Could they be trying to say: 'We are your mothers and fathers …'[11]

After the bread and soup, Margulies was led back to the barracks where it had been agreed he could sleep. He had entered a madhouse. He talked about trying to make contact with one or two women in the camp but there seemed no point in trying anything until the morning. He was told of an incident that had occurred only a few weeks before. Some of the SS officers had engaged in an orgy with some twenty or so of the prettiest young women in the camp. They had decided to allow them to live in the SS quarters as cleaners but when the women rebelled they were taken out and shot.

The barracks were controlled by an *Ordners* (elder), who was responsible for maintaining discipline. They filed past him to the bunks that lined each wall. These were three plain wooden shelves, about a metre and a half deep, that sloped down towards the wall. Each level was barely half a metre above the other, so it was impossible to sit up once inside the bunk. There were no mattresses, no sheets, no pillows. Just plain boards separated by a gap of a couple of centimetres. The bunks were so crowded that everyone had to sleep on their side. During the night, most were too weak to drag themselves out of the bunk and make their way to the night bucket, so those on the lower bunks were often woken by a shower of urine. The lights-out was at ten o'clock.

Chapter XI

When Margulies failed to return to the storm basin the following night they assumed the worst. There had been too many occasions in the past when people had gone out to the street and were never heard of again. The following day they half expected Socha to deliver news that Korsarz had been found dead somewhere near the opening to the Peltwa. But Socha had nothing to report. He sat and shared coffee with them, talked about what rumours he had of the war and left to get on with his duties. Klara was left not knowing, her anxiety unresolved: 'If he was alive, I couldn't think how he could ever find his way back to the place where we were hidden. It was impossible.'

Life continued as it had done before. While some people's thoughts were with the pirate, other matters came to a head. Genia Weinberg, the quiet member of the group, had decided she could no longer keep her condition a secret. By the middle of the month, she had begun to feel weak and had once or twice almost passed out. While the men were preoccupied with other things, she confessed to some of the women that she was about to have a baby. Though some had come to suspect it, the hard reality still came as a shock. 'I just couldn't imagine how during all our escapes, our mad scrambles, crawling through narrow pipes, how she and the foetus had survived. She had never complained of pain,' recalled Paulina.

The men were told and they too were shocked. It was the last thing they had expected. So far as Genia could tell, she was near to nine months pregnant. Chiger tried to think what should be done about it but confessed that he was 'frankly confused'. Some of the group seemed more concerned about what Socha and Wroblewski might say when they were told, and that seemed to jolt him into action. Chiger decided that he and his wife would break the news.

When Socha was told, he wavered between incredulity and outright fury. Wroblewski threw his hands into the air and refused to have anything more to do with it at all. Socha peppered them with questions: 'A baby born in the sewers? But how do you expect to deliver it? How are you going to care for it, feed it, keep it quiet …?'

No one knew the answers and the sewer workers were faced with blank expressions. Yet, no matter how much he protested, it was now an unavoidable fact that just had to be digested and somehow dealt with. And though he lectured them that it was madness to think that they could deliver a baby and then keep it alive in the sewers, he was already looking for a solution. In private, Socha talked it over with Wroblewski and between them they decided to try and find someone to adopt the baby. Perhaps even Wanda would look after it. In fact there were many possible answers, but in the meantime, of course, the baby had to survive the birth. Socha searched about for anything that might have been useful in the delivery. He decided not to go to the chemists because that would arouse suspicion and in the event was only able to find a pair of old rusty scissors and a clean towel.

Inside the Janowska camp, Margulies rose at dawn and dragged himself from the bunk. He lined up with everyone else to wait his turn at the latrine, then taking his kettle he followed the others to the kitchen. The corpses were still in the tank. Inside the kitchen, Margulies moved from one person to another, whispering to them, 'Is there a Manya Keler still here?'

Finally he came to someone who had some contact with the women's barrack. They promised to find out. He also asked after his two brothers, who had been sent to the camp the year before. There was no news of any Margulies, they must have disappeared months ago. Korsarz then had to follow his group out to the assembly ground, where they would be counted before leaving for the factory. If there was any news of Manya, it would have to wait until evening. In the factory Margulies explained to the man he had left behind that he needed to go back again at the end of the shift. They argued about the risks but Margulies was adamant about returning to the camp. At the end of the shift, they assembled once more into their familiar ranks and were marched back down the Janowska Road. Back inside the compound there was news: there was a Manya Keler and a message had been sent to her. It might be possible to get her to meet him by the wire sometime tomorrow.

As Margulies lay down on the filthy bunks in the men's barracks, back in the storm basin Genia Weinberg's labour was well advanced. She had woken the others with her soft little cries and this set in motion a remarkable scene of silent industry. All the lamps were primed and lit and a pot of water was placed on a stove to boil. The men cleared a space on the boards and lifted Genia on to them. Chiger dropped the scissors into the water and then took a small bowl of it to wash his hands and arms. He had been elected the midwife.

Old Mrs Weiss sat down beside Genia, calming her with quiet words, while Halina, who had formed a deep attachment to the woman, held her hand and applied a cool piece of cloth to her forehead. With each successive cramp, Halina took the pain in the grip of Genia's hand. Genia hardly uttered a sound. She knew that by having allowed the pregnancy to go its full course she had created a very dangerous situation for everyone. What if she were to cry out during her labour – and what of the baby's cries? She had risked all of their lives.

In fact, Genia displayed the most extraordinary resolve. Her pain intensified, and Halina could feel it through her grip. She leaned forward and whispered to her, 'Bite my shoulder. Don't make a sound, but if the pain is too much, bite into my shoulder.'

Her agonies continued for almost an hour, until finally, weak with the exertion, Genia Weinberg delivered a surprisingly weighty baby boy. His lusty cries soon filled the room. Chiger used the scissors to cut the umbilical cord and clear away the placenta. The baby was wrapped in the clean towel and handed to his mother. Yet, in the after-glow of relief and joy that spread throughout the group, there were already many who were afraid for the future. Chiger recorded that at the time he had thought to himself, 'Here we bring this new life into a sewer, where every-one else is waiting for death.'

The birth of the baby was one of the most significant episodes their entire ordeal. It brought everyone to a level of intimacy they have probably not shared since, nor may ever wish to. For some it caused certain bonds to be strengthened, for others it was devastating. It marked the beginning of what Chiger and others have described as 'the family'. However, perhaps because the incident left such a deep impression, the telling of it poses some problems. For at this point the accounts differ somewhat, though the conclusion remains precisely the same.

In the account that has come down from Mrs Weinberg herself, the story concludes as follows:

> The group quickly realized the hopelessness of trying to care for a baby under their circumstances. The baby's cries would alert people in the street of their presence and so it was agreed, unanimously, that the baby be terminated. It was taken away, killed, and disposed of.

However, the account, as recalled and recorded by the Chigers, and confirmed by Klara presents a far more tragic set of events. The baby was being held by old Mrs Weiss, while Paulina warmed some drinking water and a little sugar to try and feed it. Mrs Weinberg showed no sign of wanting to suckle the baby, so, in order to quieten the little boy's cries, Paulina tried to feed him some sweet water. She dipped a piece of clean material in the water and placed it against the baby's mouth. Instinctively, he began to suck. The baby was finally placed down beside Genia and here Chiger allowed himself a little speculation: 'The mother was apparently agonizing within herself over whether to give in to her instincts or sacrifice the child for the sake of the group ...'

The baby had been given to Genia to hold but she appeared uninterested in it. Kristina, who was seven years old at the time, recalled: 'I remember seeing my mother crawling towards the baby and trying to give it a little water, and Mrs Weinberg was taking the baby away from my mother. I saw my mother fighting with her, my mother was trying to give some water and Mrs Weinberg was pulling the baby away.' And Chiger's account records: 'She began to hug the baby closer and closer to herself, covering its face

150

with a towel or rag, supposedly to quiet the sound of his whimpering. But my wife realized that she was in fact trying to suffocate the baby and she tried to pull the cloth away.'

The struggle continued for some time until the two women were just too exhausted to continue. Paulina put her children back to bed and then laid down beside them. In the morning, the little corpse was lying beside his mother, who had fallen into a sullen trance. 'In the end, Mrs Weinberg had her way and during the night the baby had been suffocated,' wrote Chiger. It was decided they should remove the corpse quickly, before the sight caused any more distress than was necessary. Klara and Berestycki volunteered. It was an exhausting business. Klara crawled into the Seventy feet first, then the bundle was slid in and Berestycki followed afterwards. They shuffled down the pipe on their elbows, gripping the tied ends of the baby's shroud in their teeth. As they made their way down the pipe, the little corpse swung in its hammock all the way to the Peltwa.

Some time later Socha arrived ready to discuss his plans, but he was too late. Events had overtaken him. 'The baby was dead and the body already disposed of,' wrote Chiger.

Though Socha was clearly horrified by what had happened there was nothing that he could do about it. Nor could he blame anyone. He developed a tender affection for Genia, and came to look upon her as one of the more tragic victims of these events. As Chiger recorded, 'He was filled with pity for her.'

I have presented both versions simply to emphasize that there can be no absolute version. There are no independent sources. This account relies entirely on the recollections of many different people. As a footnote to her recollection of the incident, Paulina was reminded of what Mrs Weinberg had said to her at the very beginning of their ordeal in the sewers: 'Are you crazy? You bring

151

children into a place like this? Are you crazy? You cannot bring children here.'

Margulies had arranged a rendezvous with Manya at a point on the wire that divided the two compounds. At the appointed time she emerged from the women's barrack and made her way to the wire. At first she couldn't remember who he was, then he mentioned Klara, telling her that Klara was alive and well, and missed her very much. He described how badly her sister felt about abandoning her. Manya wasn't bitter. It was a difficult scene and inconclusive.

Margulies had decided from the outset that if she was alive, he would try and rescue her – and anyone else if possible. But after the little time he had spent behind the walls, he had given up this plan. The women and children in the camp were never allowed beyond the confines of the outer wall. They did not march to any outside factory and so there was no hope of escape. Margulies and Manya knew this as they spoke to each other through the wire. They agreed to meet again the following day, Manya would give him a letter. After the brigades had been assembled, he marched into the outside world again, and returned at the end of the day.

The following morning he met again with Manya and she slipped him the letter for Klara. In it she explained to Klara, '… that none of it was her fault. She wasn't to worry, besides no one could live in a sewer.'

But before Margulies could take his leave, he was suddenly assaulted by a madwoman. A figure had emerged from the women's barracks and stumbled up to the wire where Manya and Margulies stood.

'Where is my husband? Where is my husband?' she screamed.

It was Weiss's widow, completely mad. Mad with the scenes of horror she had witnessed since she and her husband had parted.

'How could he leave me to this place? How could he abandon me?'

Margulies only gradually realized who the woman was and what she was talking about. Chilled, he remembered the scene in Weiss's room when it seemed everyone wanted to get down to the sewers and Weiss's wife would not be stirred. She began screaming, louder and louder.

'Where is my husband? How could he leave me here?'

Margulies was terrified that her screaming would attract attention and that he would then be discovered. He tried to calm her but she would not be quiet. Finally he confronted her.

'Mrs Weiss, your husband is dead!' he told her. 'Your husband is dead!'

Realizing he would not be able to make himself understood, he knew that he had no option but to get away from her as quickly as possible. He ran from the wire, leaving her screaming for her husband.

Margulies was very bitter about not being able to save any of the women and children inside the camp. All that he had for his efforts was a letter from Manya. He realized, sadly, that his only realistic choice was to return to the sewers and do what he could to survive there. His presence within the camp, though shrouded in secrecy, left a residue of rumour that spread amongst the inmates. A survivor who escaped from the camp in November, recalled the stories he had heard:

Well, being in the camp I heard of some group who were hiding in the sewers. Evidently, they said, about fifteen to twenty people. And they said there were some brave Poles who worked in the sewers, that knew the sewers well and helped the Jews to hide and brought them food. That's what I heard in the camp – that some people were in hiding; how they did it I don't know, but I remember the event.[12]

During the following day's shift in the factory, Margulies spoke with the Sukakhan brothers who had looked after him during his stay. 'I said we need two strong fellows like you down in the sewer, there's plenty of work to do. But they wouldn't come with me. "We're going to die anyway, who wants to die in a sewer," they said.'

When Margulies returned to the storm basin, some four or five days after having left for the street, he was greeted like a man returned from the dead. He ignored their surprise and immediately launched into a description of where he had been and what he had seen. He delivered the letter from Manya and explained that there was nothing he could have done to help them. Then, when he had finished everything he had to say, someone told him about Genia's baby. It sobered the return of their hero. And in the morning, it was his turn to fetch the water.

Chapter XII

October was the month of the High Holidays. The New Year, Rosh Hashanah, and about ten days later, the Day of Atonement, Yom Kippur. It was a time of prayer, a time when they were reminded of the families they had lost or that had been taken from them. They were filled with memories of another age. But it was during the High Holidays that they heard the worst news from Socha. There had been reports that massive exterminations were taking place near the Janowska camp.

Rising up behind the camp is a small hill. On the near side, the side that slopes down into the grounds of the camp, was the location of the old sand quarry, Piatski. It was said that thousands of people from the camp had been taken there to be executed. It was as though the barbarities that had occurred during the liquidation of the ghetto were being revisited, all over again. In fact it was a time, though no one in the sewer would have known it, when right across the length and breadth of Nazi-occupied eastern Europe, the architects of the Final Solution seemed to have taken the High Holidays as their cue for igniting '… the crashing fires of Hell'.

The brigades that had for months been unearthing mass

graves in the sands and heaving the remains on to massive pyres, were themselves being dispatched. The pyres smouldered day in and day out, while men and women were lined up and executed with cold efficiency. Over the weeks, the ruthless *Aktion* had deteriorated into an orgy of death. This account is from Leon Wells in his book *The Death Brigade:*

> The victims undress quickly, wanting to get it over with as fast as possible, to save themselves from prolonged torture. Sometimes a mother will undress herself but will fail to undress the child. Or the child refuses to let herself be undressed out of panic … [If the child cried out in protest] the German police takes hold of the child by its small feet and swings it, crushing its head against the nearest tree, then carries it over to the fire and tosses it in.[13]

Tens of thousands of corpses were consumed, the bones crushed in a specially designed mangle, the ashes spread on the surrounding fields and the fields seeded with grass.

All the work was carried out in the greatest secrecy, and any trespassers in the area would have been shot had they been discovered. Yet the scale of the operation was such that there would certainly have been witnesses. Rumours spread through the city and reached the ears of Socha and his colleagues.

Socha delivered the report not as hearsay, but as cold hard fact. He also reported that a small camp located out by the aerodrome, where people were used as slave labour for the Luftwaffe, had been completely liquidated. Paulina had a brother who died there. Margulies, of course, was reminded of all the faces he had seen during his brief visit. For Klara it must have been the cruelest news, having heard so recently that her sister was alive. But her pain was tempered slightly by having the letter and her sister's forgiveness. Klara gave most people the impression of being a hearty and willing worker, ready to turn her hand to any job if it meant their survival. She confessed that she had been terrified throughout the ordeal and that that was what drove her to work so hard. Chiger described her as 'good natured and eager for laughter, but at the same time, easily frightened and superstitious.'

Yet, despite her fears, Klara developed a powerful self-reliance that was a source of strength to others. She used to spend a great deal of her time on her own, going for walks through the sewers. Sometimes she would take the children with her, but often she was more than content with her own company.

I was walking on my own one day and I could smell soapy water. It was not perfume, but I could still smell soap. I walked ahead and eventually found the small hole above my head that was running soapy water from a laundry. So, as I was on my own, I undressed and washed myself under this water that people had washed their laundry in. I didn't do this every week, people don't do their laundry every week in Poland. I used to have a wash like this about every four weeks …

In the streets above, the trees were losing their leaves and the cobbles were gradually being carpeted in a swath of bright copper. Wysoki Zamek, the great hill that frowns over the city, had shed its green cover and been transformed into a thicket of silver grey. The air had a fresh crispness and the towns-folk had begun queuing for rations of coal. From the countryside, woodmen were bringing cartloads of firewood to be sold by the roadside.

Paulina, like most of her companions, dreaded the approach of

winter. 'Every month that went by; two months, three, four …
How long will it last?' She woke once, during the dead of night,
and could feel the air cold against her cheek, her breath vaporizing
before her. Someone else was awake, she could hear them breathing. A harsh, rasping breath, like someone gasping for air. Paulina
got up and stole quietly across all the sleeping bodies to Mrs Weiss.
Her asthma was much worse since the temperature had dropped.

'She took my hand and I told her, "Hush, Babsha, hush. Try
and rest,"' Paulina recalled. But the old woman was at the end
of her strength.

She whispered, 'Pepa, God will help you …' The young woman
watched her pass away: 'And she died. With my finger I closed
her eyes and put the cover over her head. I decided not to do
anything but try and go back to sleep.'

In the morning Margulies roused everyone from their slum-
bers when he discovered that old Mrs Weiss was dead. As he was
about to break the news to everyone, Paulina explained how Bab-
ska had died in her arms during the night. Margulies broke the
news to Socha when he arrived at the entrance to the Seventy.

'Is the body in the room there with you?'

'Yes, of course.'

'Get rid of it. I won't come through until the body is gone.'

According to Chiger: 'Although Socha was in many ways a
fearless man, he was terribly superstitious. He could face almost
any living adversary, but would not enter a room in the presence
of a corpse.' Margulies and Berestycki did what they could to
shroud the body in some pieces of cloth and they then dragged
and pushed their burden slowly down the Seventy. They carried
it as far as the Peltwa where they slid it into the waters.

Socha's relationship with the group was the cornerstone of the entire ordeal. He occasionally explained his feelings about the work he was doing, and in doing so revealed a little of his personality. He used to describe in very moving tones the story of his seeing Paulina for the first time: 'When I squeezed through the shaft, into the little cellar, you were sitting there with Krisia and Pawel under each arm. Like a mother kite and her chicks.' He nicknamed Paulina 'Kania', which means mother kite. 'It was at that moment, when you were sitting there with the children, at that moment I decided to save you.' He used grand, demonstrative language which aroused their curiosity. 'I believe this is my mission. That I have been asked to do this, to atone ...'

It was inevitable that all the members of the group grew deeply fond of him. 'I know that he loved my son, and he loved Krisia too,' recalled Paulina. The moment he arrived, he would go to the children to see how they were and would spend time playing with them, producing little gifts that brightened their eyes. Everyone developed their own individual relationship with him, separate and unique. Each felt their own special bond. Margulies and Socha were of one mind on many things. They both seemed to understand the language of the *demi-monde*, the way to cut corners, the way to get things done; and Socha had great respect for Korsarz's talent for survival. According to Chiger, 'He liked the pirate because he was reminded of himself. Someone who was very direct and honest in his dealings – and a very hard worker.'

His relationship with Berestycki was of a spiritual kind. They were both devoutly religious. Berestycki had great knowledge of the scriptures and Socha would enjoy hearing him recite them aloud. Though anti-Semitism amongst simple Polish Catholics was virtually endemic, there seems to have developed between these two men an ecumenical link, based upon nothing more substantial than a profound devotion to the spiritual.

His relationship with Chiger was built on mutual respect. The day they first met, when Chiger had handed him a large wad of money, was a major turning point in Socha's life. Both men knew that the money could so easily have been pocketed and then Chiger and his friends been simply handed over to the authorities. It was as though for the first time someone had trusted Socha or shown respect for his integrity, especially someone like Chiger. A man of learning, a man of some standing in the community – albeit during another time. Socha had been given more than just money, he had been given the respect of a gentleman and that simple transaction caused Socha to look beyond the fact that Chiger and his friends were outlaws. What Chiger saw as a bond between one honest man and another, Socha saw as something much more substantial. According to Paulina, 'He would sit and talk with my husband about his problems. He never did anything until he had Chiger's advice on it, no matter what the subject.'

Chiger's trust was about to be tested once more. By the end of October everyone's money had been used up, including Chiger's. He had long since wished he'd struck a better bargain with Socha and claimed he had 'mistakenly assumed the war would be over by the end of the year'. Having discussed the situation with Pepa, he decided he had only one course of action.

Chiger sat down with Socha and explained the situation and then went on to describe how soon after the German occupation, before he and his family were moved to the ghetto, he had hidden a small fortune in gold and jewellery – as a sort of retirement plan, 'in case we should be lucky enough to return there after the war'. Most of the gold had been an inheritance from Paulina's family and it was all they had in the way of real wealth. He was proposing to tell Socha the location of the gold, and ask him to retrieve it. When the idea was put to him, Socha agreed without hesitation.

Before the family was evicted from the house in Kopernica Street, opposite the cinema, Chiger had buried all their valuables beneath the floor of the cellar. Socha gave the project a great deal of thought and even brought a map of the area to help them plan their approach. According to Chiger:

> After Socha and Wroblewski had left, we began to discuss the plan and many doubtful questions occupied our minds. Would they be able to find it? Would they find it and not return to us? Would they themselves be discovered digging in the cellar and so lead to our discovery? Some of the group were pessimistic and thought that I was naive for proposing such a thing to these sewer workers. For my own part, I felt I had nothing to lose …

Margulies recalled that when Socha and Wroblewski turned up at the building to investigate the cellar, they were discouraged by the concierge, who claimed not to know of any reason why the sewer authority needed to inspect her cellar. When they reported this to Chiger, Margulies chipped in with a solution: 'Wait until Sunday. She's Catholic, yes? When she goes to church, go to the house then. I promise, the place will be empty.'

The following day, Socha returned and presented them all with a long sad face. He shook his head and sighed. Chiger and the others knew what to expect. Then as they dropped their heads into their hands, Socha mischievously slipped his hand into his coat, and slowly removed what he had found in the cellar. His face beaming like a child's, he handed Chiger the money and jewels. 'Every single piece was there,' claimed Paulina. Thoroughly vindicated,

Chiger gave it back to Socha for him to change for currency. The crisis had been averted.

In November the first snowfalls settled lightly on the ground. Down in the basin, the ten survivors did what most people did as the winter months drew closer. They searched for activities to fill the time that stretched out before them. How to fill the hours, the days and weeks as news from Socha told of dramatic but painstakingly slow Russian successes in the Ukraine. Though there was now no doubt about the eventual outcome, no one knew how long it might take.

Socha had taken to delivering some reading material to help them pass the time. Chiger gratefully received thick bundles of crossword puzzles torn from all the newspapers Socha could find. Both Chiger and Halina spent a lot of time writing poetry. Halina wrote much romantic verse '... expressing in a youthful way her dreams and ambitions'. Chiger's poetry took the form of satire. It was that aspect of his character that others recalled with most affection. His ability to find humour, to find a joke in every situation, even at the darkest moments. His poems retold incidents that had happened to them all, turning their recent past into a series of anecdotes. None of these poems have survived and Chiger himself didn't record any in his account. What he does mention, and others recollect also, were the little cabarets of song, satire and poetry they used to present as an after-dinner treat. Staged in the right-angle section of the basin, under the glare of a pair of carbide lamps and before a captive audience perched on the simple wooden benches.

He also used to while away the hours with young Halina, playing a game they called 'Intelligentsia'. They would write down a long word and try and see how many other words they could make up out of the letters of the first. This resulted in many arguments about the rules and who had won, which amused some and annoyed others. Paulina recalled: 'I had no time to play these games. I had my husband to look after and the children. I wasn't alone like Halina, Klara or Jacob, I had a family …'

Though Halina seems to have been a somewhat precocious adolescent, argumentative and perhaps set apart from most of the women, she was nonetheless much loved and cared for. If she was often at odds with Chiger or Berestycki, the arguments apparently were never allowed to become serious. Chiger was also not entirely without his dark side. His temper would often get the better of his good humour and when he did become angry, it was not a pleasant sight. The most important influence in tempering any disagreements seems to have been Berestycki. In fact he had a great soothing influence on everyone's tempers, employing his quite renowned 'Hasidic witticisms' to quell the rages.

However, there was one man in particular whose personality became extremely difficult to contend with. Although Orenbach was no more than a metre and a half in height, his character more than made up for it. Somewhere deep within his experience there had developed a strangely cruel, at times even monstrous, character. His rows with Chiger and Margulies were legendary and sometimes went on for weeks. He seemed to set himself upon a particular opinion and found it impossible to accept another's point of view. 'Chaskiel was always right. He never agreed with anyone and he never let us forget it,' recalled Margulies. His tempers sometimes turned into uncontrollable furies, leaving him shaking with rage, which terrified the children, especially Kristina: 'I hated him. He was a sadist. When we were in the cavern beneath Our Lady of the Snows, I had to sleep between my father and Chaskiel. I used to dread the night,

163

having to sleep so close to him.'

His daughter, born after the war, described his character:

He was very difficult. He argued with everyone, this little one and a half metre man, always arguing. And he could be very violent – physically. But he was also very generous. He gave away his suits and shirts to people who needed them and sometimes he would come home with total strangers, to give them shelter. I think he just needed to be loved.

Orenbach had lost both his wife and three children before the liquidation of the Julag. After the birth and death of Mrs Weinberg's baby, Orenbach had started looking after the woman. It was an odd attachment, he short and irritable, she tall and quite disarmingly beautiful. Though Orenbach claimed to have taken to Genia in order to protect her after her ordeal, some of the others saw the relationship the other way round: it was he that clung to her. Whatever the case, there was considerable sympathy for Genia Weinberg and her troubled relationship with this man.

After one particular bitter row between Chaskiel and Korsarz, Kristina and the others managed to extract some small measure of revenge. Though the subject of the argument had long been forgotten, Orenbach had typically refused to have anything further to do with Margulies. He even refused to speak to him. Now, Margulies had done a little barbering before the war and one of the duties he willingly undertook in the sewers was to give everyone a regular haircut. Orenbach had begun to look quite shaggy and, though he was embarrassed by his appearance, he refused to allow Margulies to cut his hair. So Kristina offered to do it.

What began as a simple exercise, developed into a delightful little piece of theatre. Having agreed to allow Krisia to clip his locks, Orenbach brusquely indicated with his finger where she should start. She placed Margulies's shears at the appropriate point and as she began to clip away, she sang a familiar Russian folk song. The song, now forgotten, gradually ascends in scale, and as she sang higher and higher, she also ran the shears higher up Orenbach's scalp. The others sat about watching this, trying their best to control themselves. When she had finished, Orenbach was virtually bald.

Gradually it became clear that time was as much their enemy as the elements. Paulina started teaching Kristina the alphabet and Socha borrowed one of his daughter's early reading books for her to practise with. Kristina later declared: 'I never forgot the first page, *Anna ma Kota* – Anna has a cat. There was a little drawing of the girl and her cat ...' Socha also found a partly damaged prayer book amongst the ruins of the ghetto, which he gave to Halina. Klara recalled:

> I think Halina had a book, perhaps one or two books. We didn't have any knitting or anything to occupy our hands. We just sat around and talked a lot. We told stories, about ourselves and what had happened. We had to do something to occupy ourselves, otherwise we'd have lost our minds.

Naturally many of the. hours were devoured with long and detailed accounts of each others' lives. Curiously, it was Socha's stories about himself during his morning visits that turned out to have been the greatest revelation. To their utter amazement, the gentle, beaming round-faced man admitted that before he had taken up his commitment to them he had been nothing less than a common criminal. Chiger recorded Socha's revelations.

Little is known about his parents except that he'd come from a very poor background and been forced out on to the streets to fend for himself at a very early age. He had begun stealing from the age of ten and had been arrested for theft on countless occasions. He claimed that in nearly all cases when he'd fallen into the hands of the law it had been due to bad luck or betrayal. If he had learnt one thing from his career of crime, it was the value of loyalty.

As he got older his criminal exploits became more daring. He remembered having had his name and picture in the paper after a particularly notorious bank robbery. In fact, most of the others in the room could remember it too and their incredulity turned to horror.

As Socha talked further he began reeling off more of his exploits, causing his audience more and more distress. He admitted to having been in prison three times – but only because someone had betrayed him. He also claimed he had never himself betrayed anyone else: 'I would rather take the blame, than implicate others.' It probably explained why he was so familiar with the inside of Lonsky prison.

He also mentioned a particularly daring theft at a jewellery store in the district down by the main railway station. Paulina could hardly believe it.

'That was my aunt and uncle. That was their jewellery store.'

There was a great deal of nervous laughter.

'They never caught us. The crime has remained unsolved, until today.'

Socha's purpose in revealing so much of his sordid past was to try and explain his devotion to those around him. He claimed that he was motivated by a need for redemption. According to Chiger:

166

It was repentance for all the crimes he committed during his very stormy and unethical past. It was contrition, a plea for the forgiveness of God. It was his greatest mission … [There had been] a metamorphosis in his soul, as he witnessed the tragedies that had befallen the people from the Julag. He believed it was a way of snatching his sins from his soul, just as he was snatching us from certain death.

The Chigers believed these explanations completely but they never understood just how much Socha had been tempted. After he had returned the gold and jewels Chiger had hidden, Socha found an opportunity to speak quietly with Berestycki. Apparently using Berestycki as a kind of father confessor, Socha admitted that the moment he'd laid his hands on the fortune his first instinct was to take it. He claimed that he had decided to keep it and never return, but was tortured by the thought of them alone in the sewers. Right up to the last moment before returning to the sewers, he still didn't know what to do. Berestycki was of the impression that Socha never did fully understand why he was carrying on with it.

One thing is certain, his past career had fully prepared him for this secret work. Moreover, he was politically active as well. He was a socialist, a patriot and a member of the secret National Army. Though he had links with a number of partisan groups, he had little sympathy with the communists. In political terms, he barely distinguished between the Soviet Union and Nazi Germany. He claimed they were equally responsible for the rape of his country.

One morning Socha crawled through the Seventy and surprised Krisia and Pawel by removing from his bag a handful of snow.

Winter had settled in and it was time to make some form of major preparation for the months ahead. Socha had secured from a Ukrainian farmer a large cart full of potatoes, enough to last them well into next year, if they could be brought down to the sewers. He talked the proposition over with the men in the basin. They decided that the quickest way to dispose of them was to dump the lot into a manhole in the street. But how was Socha to do this without attracting suspicion? They came up with a truly artful solution.

Socha loaded up the cart with all the potatoes and then with a bag of chalk he dusted them all over with the white powder. Then he wheeled the cart to a manhole, right in the middle of the junction between Serbska and Watova Street. There he lifted the cover and began pouring the potatoes straight down the hole. Just as had been expected, people began crowding round. They couldn't understand what he was doing.

'Are you crazy? There are enough potatoes there to feed my family for six months.'

'This is a crime, you must be stopped ...'

But Socha was at his most officious.

'Stand back, don't touch. These are all condemned. They are unfit for human consumption.'

Even when two Germans approached to investigate this apparently flagrant waste, Socha was equal to the challenge.

'They have been dusted with lime, don't touch them. They are condemned. I have instructions to dump them straight into the sewers.'

'Condemned?'

'Don't touch the lime, you'll be burned. Stand back please ...'

To retrieve this manna all Margulies and Berestycki had to do was crawl down the Seventy that ran under Serbska Street. They brought all the potatoes and stored them in the basin. Naturally the rats feasted for days, but eventually they became bloated and lost interest. It was a change to see their obsession momentarily diverted from the bread.

Chapter XIII

December and January were desperate and sombre months. Time passed tortuously slowly through the heart of winter, pushed along by hours and hours of conversation which often turned into reverie. Stories from their pasts, incidents that tumbled forth and helped to strengthen the bonds of this 'family'. For the telling of stories served to do more than just devour the time. It was an opportunity to take stock of their lives, to remind themselves of who they were, where they had come from, and how they had come to be huddled under the streets of Lvov. Doubtless they heard the same stories from some people again and again, while others revealed nothing at all.

Halina's story was told both in poems that she composed in her solitude and with countless anecdotes. She enjoyed regaling an audience gathered round the bubbling soup.

Halina had been born Fayga Wind, in 1922, in the town of Turka, about 120 kilometres south-west of Lvov, in the northern foothills of the Carpathian mountains. She was the only daughter of Joshua, a watchmaker, and his wife Hannah. Joshua had a reputation within the town as a deeply religious Hasid, whose opinion, we are told, was sought on all matters by the townsfolk.

Within an extremely conservative and orthodox Jewish community, Joshua had taken the highly improper decision to send his daughter and two sons to the best private school in Turka, the secular Josef Pilsudski Gymnasium.[14] The young Wind was the only Jewish girl in the school and, though she made friends with many of the Christian children, there was nonetheless deep resentment amongst her classmates about her being allowed to graduate.

Her younger brother Leon had briefly studied at the University at Lvov, but after having endured violent attacks against his presence, he emigrated to the United States, where he studied at the Jewish Theological Seminary of America in New York. Early in 1939, he wrote to his sister Fayga, urging her to apply to the Seminary's Teachers' Institute. She applied and was admitted. By September 1939, when she had finally received her passport and was ready to leave, German forces had already swept across the Polish border and were still advancing as Soviet forces approached from the east. The Winds were woken by the sounds of bombardment, as German aircraft reached Turka before the Soviets. According to the Wind account: 'They looked out their window to the courthouse on the hill. The courthouse janitor, standing on the hill with a rifle, was shooting at an airplane, as people mocked him in the street. For Fayga, he would become symbolic of Poland's disintegration ...'

The Germans left Turka to the Soviets, who occupied it and the rest of eastern Poland until June 1941. When the Germans returned, the Nazis introduced the same regime of imprisonment and murder that had been practised throughout the rest of occupied Europe. By the autumn of 1942 there were but three Jewish families left in Turka: 'Zeeman the tailor, Brohner the shoemaker and Wind the watchmaker.' By then, these three

171

families had come to realize that they too would soon be killed and decided to try and send forth one of their number, in the hope that they might survive. Fayga was chosen as she spoke excellent Polish and knew the Catholic prayers from school. She would assume a new identity, leave the town and somehow try and escape.

On 10 November, the young nineteen-year-old, stepped out of her family house. She was now Halina Naskiewicz. She carried false papers that claimed her parents' names were John and Mary, and wore a medallion of the Virgin that her mother had given to her. Her father urged her to try and get to America, '… survive … and tell the world what happened.'

Halina took the train to Lvov where she rented a room from a Mrs Szczepaniak, a widow with two daughters. Living in the Aryan district, she daily witnessed the parade of brigades of workers from the ghetto or the camp, to the factories and back, wretched groups, clothed in rags and almost dead on their feet. While in the evening, she listened to Mrs Szczepaniak complain, 'Oh my God, have they not finished them all yet?'

On Christmas day a priest came to the house to celebrate Mass in the front parlour. As she knelt with the others to receive Holy Communion, Halina committed a venal sin. She reached out to take the host in her hand instead of, as she was a woman, allowing the priest to place it on her tongue. The indiscretion led to her capture. Mrs Szczepaniak ordered her from the house, giving her another address she could move to but when Halina arrived, Ukrainian police were already waiting for her. She had been betrayed.

Though she declared her name was Halina Naszkiewicz again and again, the police beat her and took her along to the Commissariat. There she underwent the same ordeal, but now before an officer who applied a whip rather than truncheons. The officer was determined to extract a confession and thrashed her again with the whip, while Halina continued to declare herself a Christian. Finally, when she was almost exhausted with pain, the officer presented her with her death certificate to sign. Halina thought, 'He'll beat me until I do … they'll kill me anyway.' She signed.

Then she was taken to a cell where she slept fitfully, listening to the screams of others. With the dawn she was woken again and ordered outside. There she joined a group of 'false Aryans' who were being loaded on to the little open tram waggons that ran down the tram tracks. They were driven through the town to the gates of the Ghetto, unloaded and marched inside to the prison on Weisenhof Street.

Her first impressions were recorded: 'Inside the stench was unbearable. The place was filthy, the people like shadows. Buckets served as toilets. A guard told her, "It's your turn to empty the buckets."' Halina took hold of a bucket of excrement and walked down the corridors. Ahead of her she could see daylight from the courtyard; someone had left the main door wide open. There being no sign of any guards she walked out into the courtyard, still carrying the bucket. She looked around herself and saw that she was alone. It was a beautiful day, quiet and still. She put the bucket down and walked straight for the gates to the prison and slipped outside.

Out in the streets of the ghetto, she pressed herself against the walls and waited. The streets were empty. Though she did not know it, everyone was either at work, or in hiding. Halina walked slowly down to Peltewna Street and from there headed towards the railway embankment. In the prison, the alarm had been raised and the dogs had been alerted. Terrified and still dazed with pain, she pressed herself against another wall; it was the barrack under the shadow of the railway line. Suddenly she heard a voice speak in Yiddish.

'Come in! Come in!'

A man had slipped out of a doorway and taken her by the arm. Halina was now even more terrified.

'You're from the prison.'

'How do you know?'

'They're already coming for you. Come inside.'

Halina refused. She had no way of knowing who to trust any more. Then she heard the voice of an elderly woman.

'Come in, don't be afraid.'

Uncertain what to do, she allowed herself to be led inside, down a corridor, into a room. There she met another man, short and agile, who introduced himself as Jacob. The two who had led her off the street were Weiss and his mother. Still terrified of some retribution, Halina complained that she wanted to get back to the prison, but she was finally reassured.

'Don't worry,' whispered Berestycki. 'You can stay with us. We'll get you the correct papers so that you can work.'

Finally reassured, Halina agreed to stay. Weiss and his wife found space on their floor for her to sleep beside their daughter and the old woman. She was visited every day by Berestycki, who brought her food – and eventually the papers of someone recently deceased; occupation: Seamstress. With these papers she had automatically joined the ranks of women who daily marched to and from the Schwartz und Comp. factory. She was alive, she had work, she had a place to stay and the company of Jacob and Weiss's family. That had all taken place a year ago ... [15]

Every Friday, when Socha collected his money, he reminded

them in a somewhat unnerving way that their financial resources were finite and that he and his fellows would eventually have to cease their visits.

'I don't know what will happen. They will not work for nothing,' he would say. These reminders would come without warning, 'like a dark cloud' casting them all into depression. 'It will be very difficult when the money runs out and you can no longer pay for the *last cutlet*.' A curious phrase he used to repeat.

With this sword of Damocles above their heads, they got on with adapting to the new freezing conditions. They burned the kerosine stoves for heat, but were forced to shut everything off every now and again because the stoves were using up all the air. They slept on top of one another to keep warm, and the youngest developed all manner of ways to win favours in order to keep warm. According to the Weinberg account:

> Pawel used to sing, inventing the tune to his song, but always the same words, 'Please, Mrs Weinberg, can I sleep beside you …' He also used to collect cigarette ends that had been washed down from the gutters. Then he would dry them out somewhere and trade them in return for being allowed to curl up beside her.

As the temperature dropped their little room became very damp. Condensation from their breathing and the regular use of the kerosine stoves meant that the walls ran with water, the floor became soaked and, at night, a thin sheet of ice was formed on the ground. This dank atmosphere suddenly evaporated one evening as Mrs Weinberg set about preparing the evening meal. Chaskiel Orenbach had offered to fire up the stoves for Genia and was sitting crouched on his knees, pumping up the pressure in the kerosine cylinder. Margulies recalled:

> These stoves needed careful maintenance. We had a little
> pin we used to unblock a tiny air hole in the top. And I said
> to this fellow Chaskiel – he was bloody stubborn, really
> bloody stubborn – I said, 'Chaskiel, when you finish, open
> the top and let out the air, otherwise the petrol shoots up.

Beside it was a stove already running, and on top a bucket of
boiling soup. Margulies continued: 'And Chaskiel – he, he just
didn't want to listen to me. Eventually it exploded. WHOOSH,
out the top – and beside it the naked flame. Suddenly there it
was all on fire.'

Chiger, who realized what had happened only after it was too
late, was alarmed that the flames and smoke might be seen from
the street. 'So we began to beat the flames with rags and cloth –
anything we had available.'

Margulies decided to pick the stove up and carry it across to
where they dumped the used carbide. He was halfway across the
room, he remembered, with the blazing stove in his hands:
'Chaskiel picked up some *shmutter*, some pillows or something to
dampen down the flames, and threw it at the stove. It knocked
the stove out of my hands and on to the floor. The fuel leaked out
and the flames took off across the floor and leapt up and up.'
The fire now roared up the walls and arched over their heads.
They were trapped in the little chamber, virtually surrounded by
fire and about to be consumed. At that point Halina got quite
hysterical and tried to climb into the narrow pipe that trickled
water from the street. She had presumed it would be some kind
of escape. Now Margulies lost his temper: 'I grabbed her and
pulled her away because she would block up the air. She was

hysterical, so I hit her. I gave her two or three hits and pulled her away. I said, "Don't block up the hole." She couldn't even remember it afterwards.'

Then Margulies and Chaskiel grabbed the shovel and trowel, scooped up the dried carbide they had dumped in the corner and threw it on to the flames. After countless trips back and forth to the carbide, they succeeded in smothering the flames. When the danger had passed they looked around at each other and saw ghostly visions of their companions. Their hair singed, their eyelashes and eyebrows gone and their faces smeared with soot. For some it was the most terrifying moment of their lives; a realistic taste of hell. Immediately there were remonstrations.

'What if Halina had saved herself and deserted us?' demanded Chiger. In fact, this would have been impossible because the pipe was too narrow to have allowed her to escape. But Chiger went on: 'Who knows what would have happened to her – and to us – if she had got up to the street?'

However, once the mess had been cleaned up and they were able to sit and reflect, Chiger cheered them up.

'You look liked smoked herring,' he declared. 'Like what the English call kippers. A row of kippers!'

During October, Socha had been impressed by the way the group had observed their important religious festivals. In fact he had joined them to celebrate Rosh Hashanah. So when Christmas came, he was keen to share *his* most important religious festival. These celebrations, and they found innumerable other little occasions to observe as well, were usually brought to life with a little vodka. They had first shared a drink on the occasion of Paulina's birthday, which had been in July. A typical celebration would begin with Socha lacing their coffee from a bottle he kept in his coat pocket. Inevitably, one tot led to two or three more. The Catholic's taste for the hard stuff was considered a little imprudent, especially by Paulina who thought it at the least socially unbecoming and at worst, downright dangerous. Chiger claimed that he was not keen on vodka, but admitted that, in the interest of the group's overall security, he was sometimes obliged to 'drink as much as a half-litre in one gulp in order to prevent Socha and Wroblewski from getting drunk and perhaps accidentally talking loosely on their way home'.

Of course, neither Socha nor Wroblewski were drunks, but they were of a social group where alcohol played an important part in their daily lives. It is a matter of pride amongst heavy drinkers that they can hold their drink, and it's unwise for the uninitiated to suggest otherwise.

On one unfortunate occasion, Paulina, Mrs Weinberg and the children were seated on their own, around the corner from the rest of the group, who were enjoying the Polish national drink. None more so than Socha. Paulina became alarmed at Socha's state and motioned to Berestycki to come and sit beside her. When he was close by she whispered to him that perhaps he should try and talk with Socha.

'Jacob, I don't think they should drink so much. They will be going out soon, they must be careful.'

Unfortunately, she'd spoken too loudly and the good humour suddenly vanished. Socha rose to his feet and turned on Paulina. He said nothing to her directly but summoned Wroblewski to his feet and informed him in a voice that could be heard by everyone that, in the light of what he had just overheard, he would no longer enter the basin whenever the food was delivered. In future, they could crawl through the Seventy to collect it at the other end.

'Mrs Chiger doesn't trust us. She thinks we're drunk!'

The following day, and the day after, Socha whistled from the other end of the Seventy and Margulies and Berestycki had to crawl through the pipe to collect their bread. The situation continued like this for a number of days and it soon depressed them all greatly. There could not have been a more dramatic example of the power of Socha's presence and conviviality, than when they were deprived of it.

According to Paulina, 'What could I do? He was so proud. The situation was terrible. The men, Jacob and Chiger, talked amongst themselves and decided I had to apologize to Socha. So, I agreed to go with the two men when they collected the food.' Paulina crawled into the Seventy, following Margulies and Orenbach. When she emerged at the other end, Socha was in the process of handing the food across to the others. He stared at the figure struggling through the opening.

'What are you doing?' He turned, absolutely furious, upon the two men. 'How could you do this? How could you let Mrs Chiger crawl through this terrible pipe? Mrs Chiger, this is terrible what they have done …'

Paulina's appearance had not only surprised him, he was embarrassed and completely disarmed. He took refuge in an attack upon the men, who stood there completely nonplussed.

'How could you make a woman crawl all this way …?'

'But Klara crawls …'

'Mrs Chiger is a woman and a mother! Now, back you go, all of you!'

Without having been given a chance to explain, Margulies and Orenbach climbed back into the pipe and were followed by Paulina and then by Socha and Wroblewski. Once inside the room, Socha's fury knew no bounds. 'He gave them hell,' recalled Paulina.

'I will never forget this. Mrs Chiger, why did you let them make you do this?'

'You were angry with me. I couldn't live with that. It could not be so. We love you very much, you are the most important man to us – and you would not come and see us.'

Socha, doubtless deeply moved by this testament, turned again upon the men.

'I will never forget this. How you could let a woman and a mother – a mother of two children ...!'

But Paulina interrupted this continuing attack upon the menfolk.

'Socha! I apologize if you thought I was calling you a drunk.'

This had a welcome effect. Socha seemed prepared to listen further.

'It was just for our common good. That's all I was thinking of, I wasn't trying to criticize you. I saw Stefak drinking and drinking and I was afraid that when you went out ...'

Paulina, in her wisdom, had stumbled on the solution. It was really Stefak's drinking she had been concerned about. That was a different matter altogether. Socha was once again his calm, reassuring self.

'Of course, I am always careful. But Stefak ... Please don't worry. I will look after him.' The issue was forgotten and Socha continued with his visit, something he clearly enjoyed just as much as they did.

From time to time Socha would report his misgivings about Wroblewski's heavy drinking, but that he had the miscreant under the closest supervision. One day he arrived on his own and reported at great length and with much detail the latest of Stefak's indiscretions. Rolling his eyes, glancing at Paulina for confirmation and shaking his head to great effect, he explained how easily the man could go astray.

'It being Sunday I called round to see Stefak. But his wife told me he wasn't at home. "Where was he?" I asked.

'"In the bar, I think," she said.

'Well, I went straight round to the bar and there he was, sitting with his friends, drinking, chattering away.'

Poor Stefak, he must have wondered what had happened to him.

'I went straight in and grabbed hold of him and marched him all the way home again. Then I lectured him about how careless he had been, drinking with these people. What if he had let something slip? But the worst of it was that he was sitting there with the wristwatch you gave him, Mr Chiger. Now where does a simple sewer worker get such a watch?'

Socha's report, however embellished, had the desired affect. He was a man to be trusted. They were safe with Socha in control. But that Stefak, he'd have to be watched.

The winter months were filled with incidents, not many of which can be given particular dates. There was the occasion when Pawel slipped and fractured his leg, which caused everyone a great deal of anguish. Socha in particular. They apparently discussed whether Socha should take Pawel out and have him treated, but they ruled it out as being just too dangerous. They wondered if Socha might get some medicine from the pharmacy, perhaps a splint and some bandages, but this was vetoed as well, on the grounds that it might draw too much attention. In the end, Socha had to admit that they could do little for Pawel and just hope that the fracture would set perfectly with the meagre bandage they had provided. Which was precisely what happened. Chiger put it down to Pawel's 'youth and generally healthy state'.

But Pawel's health was not always so robust. At one point he contracted an infection in his throat that led to him losing his voice. Again, there was no prospect of getting any medication and once more there was serious concern that 'he was very sick'. Socha sat down with Paulina while she nursed Pawel and asked, 'What do you think will help him?'

Paulina wasn't certain, but mentioned an old wives' cure, raw eggs. Socha said no more and left soon afterwards. A few hours later:

> We heard a noise. Someone was wriggling down the pipe towards us. My father got quite scared because he couldn't imagine who would be coming. Then suddenly, I remember, his face appearing through the pipe. It was Socha beaming through clenched teeth, for in his mouth he was holding the ends of a handkerchief filled with fresh eggs. That was the sort of person he was ...'

On another more serious occasion, the problem was Kristina. She had plunged into a deep state of 'melancholy', as Chiger described it. It was more than just a depression, it verged upon a state of catatonia. She stopped eating and talking and all she wanted to do was sleep. Otherwise she sat on her own, or in her mother's arms and stared blankly off into the distance. It went on this way for almost a month, and as each day went by she grew weaker and weaker. She seemed to be dying.

Socha became quite distressed. He came to see her every day and worried constantly about her condition. One day he came on his own and took Krisia into a corner, away from the others.

He sat me on his lap and he began talking to me, quietly. He just told me stories and told me not to worry … 'Someday soon, you will breathe the air and you will see the daylight. It won't be long, you'll be like the other children and you will see the daylight … I will help you, don't worry. I am always with you and Pawel. I'm always with you …'

And he took me down the pipes, to a place where I could see daylight – probably a manhole – and he picked me up and held me up to the light and he said, breath the air and look! See the daylight …

I think it was soon after that I began, slowly, to behave normally again. I started to talk and react and eat again … It was Socha who did it.

Apart from the illnesses that they were constantly prey to, there were other, less obvious hazards they had to cope with. One day Margulies and Berestycki were off on a journey to fetch water. They were passing beneath the corner of Czarniecklego and Ruska Streets, near the bottom of the Wysoki Zamek. The streets above, being under two or three feet of snow, were regularly cleared and much of it was swept down the hill and piled up around Czarnicklego Street. Once this had been done, large chutes in the street were opened and the snow simply shovelled down into the sewers.

This had all been done without Margulies and Berestycki having been alerted. They had made their way some distance down one of the large elliptical tunnels and along the way they remarked to each other at how little water was flowing around their feet. In fact, hardly any at all. Then they heard a strange noise up ahead of them.

'Jacob, something is wrong,' Margulies said. 'Can you hear that noise?' It was a deep, dark rumbling – like a constantly erupting explosion. And it was getting louder. The snow had been dumped into the tunnel and had completely blocked it up. The pressure of the water behind it had begun to melt the snow and now it was beginning to shift down the tunnel towards them.

The two of them turned and began to run in the opposite direction. The noise behind them became deafeningly loud and seemed almost upon them. Ahead of them off to the left they spied a branch tunnel, which they leapt into. Just as they got there they had enough time to turn and see a filthy grey wall of ice and mud thunder past the opening. According to Margulies: 'It was a mountain of snow, moving like a torpedo. Just like a torpedo it was. We could not have survived in its path.'

In the midst of the gloom, there was one bright moment which probably gave cause for another of Socha's little celebrations. Throughout 1943 the Soviet armies in the Ukraine had won victory after victory, pushing the Germans from Kiev, the Kerch peninsula, the Crimea and back towards the Polish border. By the middle of January, Socha would have been able to report that on the tenth of the month the Red Army had taken the Polish town of Lyudvipol, about twenty kilometres inside the border. Of course, at that stage they had no idea it referred to the pre-1939 border, which had become nothing more than an historical remnant. The Allies had agreed at the Tehran Conference to redraw the Polish borders, ceding great tracts of pre-war Polish territory to the Soviet Union. Doubtless Socha and his companions had toasted the beginning of Poland's liberation, unaware that the Soviet armies of the Ukraine were in fact liberating what would become Soviet territory.

Despite these little scraps of news, January was a month of unremitting depression for it was then that the day they had been dreading finally came upon them. They had run out of money and somehow had to admit this fact to Socha. Although they knew that Socha was aware of this inevitability, it made everyone terribly nervous. As Chiger recalled, it was one of those harsh realities that simply could not be ignored. They unanimously agreed that it should be Paulina who broke the news.

'Socha had a very deep respect for her,' Chiger noted.

So later in the morning, once Socha had delivered the provisions, Chiger ushered the others out of the way while Paulina whispered to Socha that she wanted to discuss a most serious matter.

'What's wrong?'

'Just as you predicted, we have no more money.'

'What completely finished? Everybody?'

It was something the two of them had dreaded. It would mark the end of their relationship. Wroblewski and Kowalow had been adamant, it would be the finish.

'Well, it's very sad. You know we will have to stop coming.'

'As you like,' Paulina pronounced, as hard as she could. 'As you like. We are not coming out into the street. Whether we live or not, we're staying here.'

It was difficult for them to imagine, as he slipped down the Seventy, that his farewell had been the last they would hear. They tried to concentrate their minds upon contingency plans, foraging in the street, stealing from the market – anything that might get them through. Despite news of the Red Army's victories, they realized they were still some months away from salvation.

The following morning they woke and went about their normal routine. They had some three or four days worth of bread in the bucket slung from the roof and there were still plenty of potatoes. The coffee would run out in about a week and the little

185

condiments – salt, pepper, sugar – might last another fortnight. It was not completely hopeless, but they were unable to plan very far into the future.

Then, as they sat there sipping their coffees and nudging the same problem back and forth, there came the familiar shuffles from the other end of the Seventy. They all gathered round the opening to see who it might be. First a bag was pushed through, then another – they were Socha's. Then Socha himself emerged and stood there beaming from ear to ear. Amidst their dumb incomprehension, he handed over a few more kilos of bread and then sat down to share some coffee. Nothing seemed to have changed, except that of course he had come without Wroblewski and Kowalow.

'The others wouldn't come. They won't work for nothing.' They all stood around him, their eyes wide with expectation. 'But ... I told them that I'd go on until the job was finished. I told them I wouldn't back out.'

'But we have no money ...'

'I will go on until the job is finished.'

'And the others ...?'

'Stefak's out and Kowalow ...' He told them of a conversation he'd had with his foreman. It seemed that Kowalow had been concerned for his own skin. If the Jews had crawled out into the street in desperation and were captured they might tell the Germans about the help they'd been getting from three sewer workers.

'Kowalow said we should just poison the lot of you. Give you strychnine somehow. I told him whatever he thought, I must continue. The children must survive.'

All their words of gratitude could not properly express their true feelings. What had happened seemed miraculous. The following day he returned again with more bread and on the third day, Stefak too crawled through the pipe.

'I changed his mind for him! He's still with us!' Socha declared to his audience. Clearly, Socha saw the group as a great responsibility – a kind of mission. But Wroblewski? Perhaps Socha also had hidden evangelical powers.

As Paulina said, 'I began to think he had been sent by God. He was so honourable.' Even Kowalow eventually resumed his responsibilities, standing guard at the open manhole.

'Do what you like …' was all he was reported as saying.

On the Friday of that week, Socha established a small charade, which was to be re-enacted on the same day thereafter. Fridays had always been the day Chiger paid Socha his 'wages'. On this occasion, soon after he had entered the chamber, Socha somehow contrived to slip Chiger a roll of money.

'You'll give it to me for the week just as before. When I am about to leave.'

Paulina is certain this was done in order to save Chiger embarrassment: 'He didn't want anything to appear to have changed.' But it also seems possible that this elaborate ruse was for the benefit of Wroblewski and Kowalow, who might have been labouring under the impression that their Jews had found more money. At any rate, Socha's answer to all the doubts was always the same.

'This is my decision.'

Chapter XIV

The winter weather did nothing to impede the Soviet army's momentum. By the end of January they had recaptured Novgorod in the north and re-opened the Moscow-Leningrad railway line. By February the Red Air Force had begun bombing Helsinki, and had crossed the Estonian frontier. While down in their part of the world, the 1st and 2nd Ukrainian Armies had linked up in the southern Ukraine, trapping ten German divisions.

Socha reported every scrap of news from the war that he could glean. Chiger relished this intelligence and plotted each development on a map that had been published in one of the underground newspapers. Then he would spend hours poring over his papers like an old campaigner, before predicting the Soviet's next move. All news of German defeats gave everyone great heart, for each one brought the date of their liberation closer. The question that lingered constantly in the air was, when? For how much longer could they survive in the basin? How long could Socha maintain their security? How long before they all collapsed from the pain in their backs that had developed from constantly having to be stooped over? By the beginning of February they had been underground for eight months.

It was impossible to answer. The Soviet advances might run out of steam, the Germans might counter-attack, the war might turn again. All the possibilities were discussed and debated at great length, particularly by Chiger and there developed the general impression that it would be over very soon. This singular thought carried them through the darkest months of the winter when the ground had hardened and the pipes they had to crawl through were as cold as ice, when massive blocks of ice floated down the Peltwa and avalanches of snow descended through the manholes above.

During that winter, conditions on the street were harder than anything in living memory. Most of the coal had been commandeered and serious food shortages soon meant that the population was living on starvation rations. The streets were filled with the homeless who had come in from the countryside to find shelter and avoid starvation. Beggars stood in every street and gathered like packs of dogs around rubbish heaps outside the large military establishments – the only place where food in any quantity was always in constant supply.

One of those forced into vagrancy was a distant cousin of Margulies, Jan Felix. He claimed: 'We ate what dogs ate. We searched the dustbins for food, I even forgot the word for bread.'

The shortages made it even more difficult for Socha and his wife to feed the people below. Yet no matter how difficult life became, none of the group ever felt that it had become impossible; there seemed to be no waning in Socha's determination to see it through.

Every so often Socha would take a walk past the Bernadinski Church, just to satisfy himself that there was nothing untoward that might give them away. One day, however, he turned the corner from Serbska Street to be confronted by a chilling sight. A group of people had gathered in the middle of the road and were talking animatedly about the most curious phenomenon at their feet. The snow had melted. What was most curious was that the snow had melted in a curious 'L shape', right in the centre of the road. No one had seen anything like it. Old women had gathered and were kneeling down to touch the ground, men shuffled their boots and pulled at their ears. It was most mysterious.

Socha realized immediately what had happened and he turned on his heel and hurried as inconspicuously as possible to the nearest manhole. He clattered down the ladder and made his way to the storm basin, calling to them as he shuffled through the pipe. The group was alarmed at the tone of his voice. When he got inside, sure enough, the two kerosine stoves were blazing away and Mrs Weinberg was preparing her potato soup, just as usual.

'Shut off the stoves. You're making too much heat, the snow is melting!'

'What?'

'The snow in the street, just above. It's all melted!'

The stoves were shut down but clouds of steam still hung in the air. The walls ran with condensation and there was nothing they could do to cool anything down. Socha suggested they put the stoves in another corner of the room, immediately beneath the wall of a block of apartments. They agreed, but it never really solved the problem of the room filling with steam whenever they did any cooking. The room would inevitably warm up and continue to melt any snow in the street above.

In the meantime, Socha returned to Serbska Street to try and dispel any theories that may have taken root. Now the small crowd had been joined by one or two Germans who confronted the man wearing waterproof overalls and thigh boots. They asked the obvious question.

'Are there Jews down there?'

He remained calm and assured them there was nothing of the kind in the sewers.

'The Jews drowned or were poisoned long ago. The snow has melted from the heating pipes in the cellar of the apartment house.' He indicated with a jerk of his thumb over his shoulder. 'Or perhaps it had something to do with the monastery behind the church. The catacombs run everywhere under the road …' He left them in no doubt. 'There's no mystery, there's nothing down there …'

The voice of authority, calm and matter of fact. The enquiries passed by and so did the Germans.

These little incidents were the milestones that marked out their journey together. But as Chiger says in his account: 'I did not keep a formal diary because, although I had the time, our existence was so similar – day after day, that it need not be recounted in that way.' As he goes on to explain, the only other milestones were the stories told by each one of them in turn, 'to try and pass the time of day'. Berestycki's story was like thousands of others. He had been born in 1910, in the city of Lodz, some 100 kilometres south-west of Warsaw. Like his father before him, Berestycki was a locksmith by trade. After the German occupation, he left the city and went to live in the anonymity of a nearby village, but when the Nazi embrace reached to every little hamlet, he was forced to return to Lodz and take up the work he was assigned to. About the spring of 1942, the Judenrat in Lodz informed him that he had been assigned to the labour authorities in Lvov, where he would be put to work at the railway maintenance shops. He was transported to the Janowska camp and from there he marched out each day with a brigade of workers, to the Ostbahn workshops and back again. It was while he was kept at the Janowska camp that he met Leon Wells, a survivor whose testimony ensured the camp's immortality in his book *The Death Brigade*.

From the camp Berestycki was sent to the ghetto, to work in a maintenance shop supervised by Ignacy Chiger. Margulies recalled:

> I remember the day Berestycki turned up in the ghetto. He didn't know anyone. He was sitting on his haunches in the street, in front of a little fire. He had built it between two bricks and was heating a cup of tea. I spoke to him and he said he was from Lodz. I suggested he come into the 'barrack' and I introduced him to Weiss. He regularly took people in off the street and helped get them papers.

That was in the autumn of 1942, Berestycki was about thirty-two and, like most of his generation, confronted with the daily threat of extinction.

Perhaps one of the best storytellers amongst the group was Korsarz Margulies. He kept them entertained for hours with his tales from the early days of the war. If Margulies had not been forced to become a black-marketeer, he would probably have followed his father's trade as a land agent, or perhaps continued as a travelling salesman for his sister's factory, selling children's clothes from shop to shop.

All of that was changed in the autumn of 1939. By midnight on 1 September, the day the Germans launched their attack across the Polish border, Lvov had already received its first air attack and in the morning, railyards and factories were still blazing. Air raids followed every night and within a fortnight, German troops had penetrated to within sixty miles of Lvov. Though

Poland's defences had been swiftly overwhelmed, there were a few spirited pockets of resistance. None more heroic than the garrison led by General Sosnkowski, who had been charged with the defence of Lvov. However, just as German supply lines began to be over-stretched and heavy rain had turned the fields into quagmires, Poland's last hopes were extinguished. At 6.00 a.m. on 17 September, the Soviet Union launched its own attack from the east. At 2.00 a.m. the same morning, the Soviet government had communicated to Berlin a request for 'the German Air Force not to operate' in the area of Lvov, as the Red Air Force would begin bombing in the morning. There was nowhere for the Polish armies to retreat to; all that was left was for the large city garrisons to hold out as long as possible. By 22 September, Red Army units had reached that city, to find it all but surrendered to the Germans. A young First Secretary of the Soviet Ukraine, Nikita Krushchev, described the scene.

> If the Germans had had their way, they would have entered the city first and sacked it. But since our troops had got there ahead of them, the Germans were careful not to show any hostility towards us. They stuck to the letter of the treaty and told us … 'Please! Be our guests! After you!'[16]

The German forces withdrew and the Soviets occupied the city. Poland had been carved up between her two neighbours.

Under Soviet occupation the city was inundated by Russian and Georgian soldiers. They were like peasants let loose in an exotic bazaar; polite but dazzled by the quantity and variety of produce in all the stores. They would enter an establishment and ask if it was permissible to buy a pair of boots, and, if it was, then was it permissible to buy two pairs, or four, or six. They would take as many as they could carry. Money was no obstacle.

By mid-October 1939, the city had commenced the required programme of socialization and thousands of Soviet officials and their families arrived to organize the transformation. Large industrial complexes were nationalized as were apartment buildings and the apartments within. The management of the factories was replaced with Soviet technocrats. Small trading establishments were allowed to continue, but Margulies's sister was forced to close her factory. There would be no market for children's wear.

Nevertheless, a black market flourished. The Soviets opened their own government stores and stocked them from whatever suppliers they could find. Margulies and some friends, a Ukrainian and his sister, decided to take advantage of the situation. They opened a barber's shop. His friend knew of an empty premises near the prison. They knocked the lock off the door, and moved in. Soon they had the establishment up and running.

'He cut the men's hair, she cut the ladies'. I did all the soaping up and the finishing off,' Margulies told them. Within a month Margulies had learnt the basics of the trade, but the entire exercise had really been set up as a front to provide an official trading premises, with the documents to go with it, through which they could shift black-market goods. Business was good for everyone as just about every razor blade in Lvov had been bought up at the beginning of the occupation and no more were to be had anywhere. The black market did extremely well, but eventually, Margulies was ordered to report to the Soviet Railway Co-operative to find work. Apart from his duties in the Cooperative, he also had to attend hours of deadly boring lectures on the principles of collectivization and worker control. Margulies had endured more than an hour of one of these lectures when he decided that life was too short and slipped away. In the morning he was ordered to the commissar's office to explain his absence. Margulies explained to the man behind the desk, 'Halfway through I got terrible stomach ache and went to the toilet. When I came out, the meeting was over and everyone was gone.'

The world-weary commissar listened to this unlikely story and decided to humour Margulies. He described his very great disappointment, for Margulies had missed being awarded a prize.

'A prize? For what?'

'For your work …' The Commissar took out a 1000-rouble note and held it out before him. 'We were going to present you with this wonderful prize, which we would have been delighted to see you donate to the defence of the Soviet Union.'

Margulies could barely contain himself. The absurdity of the Russian's gambit only inspired his contempt.

'You would give me a 1000-rouble note?'

The Commissar nodded.

'Listen!' continued Margulies, 'Every week I give money to the Soviet Union. I pay fees, taxes, commissions, everything. The day I get 1000 roubles from the Soviet Union I will not give it back again. I put it in a frame and hang it above my bed!' Thankfully, both men shared the joke.

Margulies claimed he didn't mind the Soviet occupiers. He had found ways and means to get round the system they had tried to establish. Indeed, for most people, it was not a harsh occupation, though the Ukrainian population were intimidated and the nationalist elements in particular ruthlessly persecuted, imprisoned and transported.

The situation was reversed, however, when at midnight on the 21 June 1941, the Germans launched their surprise attack on the Soviet Union. Within six days, the Soviets began what they hoped

195

would be a disciplined and orderly retreat from Lvov. However, their plans were frustrated by Ukrainian fascists who blew up bridges and mined the streets to delay the Russians' escape, while snipers operated from anonymous windows. The last of the Soviet units left Lvov on 30 June and by the early hours of the following morning the first German units had arrived in the suburbs.

When the Germans made their triumphant parade into the city, they were greeted with cheering Ukrainian crowds that had lined the streets. The streets were decked with brilliant red and black swastikas and, above the two towers of the town hall, the swastika and the blue and white Ukrainian flag flew side by side. The Ukrainian population saw, at last, the arrival of a liberating army. Civilized, ordered and surely committed to the establishment of the long-awaited independent Ukrainian state. The Ukrainians volunteered in their tens of thousands to take up arms with the Germans against the great Bolshevik enemy. They also took up the racial policies of the Nazi and joined in the persecution of the Jews.

'The Germans are our enemies' enemies; so the Germans are our friends,' explained a Ukrainian friend to Margulies. These events had taken place more than two and a half years ago and by 1944 an independent Ukraine was as much a myth as it had ever been.

Margulies did his best, throughout the German occupation, to keep his head above water. His stories of the various deals he had run and the risks he had taken under the Germans' noses, were just as enthralling, if not quite so amusing, as his stories of outwitting the Russians. The Germans soon closed the barber shop and pounced on his merchandising. He was imprisoned for having tried to purchase a quantity of pilots' warm, long underwear from some Luftwaffe officers. He spent many months in Lonsky prison and his account of it rivalled any other.

Despite never having managed to get the correct papers that would have allowed him to live in the ghetto, Margulies found a room in the barracks. From there he got work at the large cloth co-operative Textalia, where, despite being an illegal worker, he did a good trade selling duplicate copies of the badges worn by the legal workforce. These little patches worn above the heart and bearing the legend 'W.R.' (denoting that the wearer was engaged in work for the Wehrmacht), were conveniently manufactured, and duplicated, at the co-operative. 'We sold hundreds of them ...' declared Margulies.

He had also established a reliable trade in fresh produce from the Ukrainian farmers. Taking his friends' clothes, money, jewellery – whatever could be spared – Margulies would seek out the farmers and trade the merchandise for food.

On one occasion I was returning to the ghetto with a bucket filled with fresh eggs, but first I scooped up a layer of horse droppings and laid it over the eggs. You see, I knew what would happen. The Ukrainian policeman says to me in the street, 'What have you got there?' I hold the bucket of horse-shit under the man's nose and tell him to see for himself. Then I am quickly into the crowd before he has time to think about it.

As life within the ghetto deteriorated, more and more people resorted to trading their belongings for food. Margulies was appalled at how trusting some of his colleagues could be; standing at the ghetto gates laden down with their finest clothes, trousers, jackets, shirts.

I saw so many people get cheated because the Ukrainians

would snatch the clothes and run. It was forbidden to chase them because if you left the ghetto you were shot. I would tell them again and again, 'Don't let go of what you have. Don't let them measure the trousers. If they measure, they're gone. Wait until you have what they can trade ...'

There was a story Chiger told many times, which Paulina too would have shared with the others. It happened during the spring of 1942. Grzymek often employed Chiger and his crew of carpenters to do private work on his own apartment. Grzymek lived in a smart block of apartments inside the confines of the ghetto. Chiger had been asked to do some work and to have it finished by a particular time. Chiger and his crew took an hour longer than instructed and Grzymek decided that, as punishment, Chiger and his entire family would be hanged. As Chiger was being led down the street, he brushed against someone he knew and managed to whisper a warning:

'Tell my wife to take the children up to the tailor's apartment on the third floor.'

When Paulina got the message she gathered up the children and ran up the stairs. When they were safely in their friend's apartment, Pawel went to the window to see the cause of a commotion in the street.

'Look, I think they are going to hang someone,' he said innocently. Paulina watched from the window as her husband was ordered to stand on a chair in the street, while a noose was placed over his head and the other end thrown over a lamp post. His wallet and other belongings in his pockets were removed. The soldiers hauled down on the rope and awaited the order from Grzymek to kick away the chair. At this point, Chiger claimed that everything went blank and he could remember no more.

However, Paulina witnessed everything from the window. As she was steeling herself for her husband's certain death, Grzymek stepped forward and simply said: 'Let him go.'

The rope was dropped and Chiger ordered off the chair. He was told to get on to his knees and thank the Nazi for saving him – which he did automatically. He said afterwards that he could remember nothing of what had happened from the moment he stepped on to the chair. The whole episode had been utterly senseless.

Kristina recalled many bright and some bleak moments from her early childhood. Going to the cinema near her house to see *Snow White* and in summer, walking with her mother up the slopes of Wysoki Zamek for a picnic. There on the hill above the city, people would come for their midday break to escape the heat of the summer. The occupation had stopped all that. Though she witnessed many terrible things, somehow she had been protected from the worst aspects of the war, right up until the beginning of 1943. That was when her grandparents – the Chigers, were taken away:

I remember, when we were living with them, in the evening I used to sing a lullaby for my grandfather. He would say, sit next to me and sing, and he would hold my hand. One day my father came home and said they were coming for the old people tomorrow. My grandfather said, you must leave now but my father would not and told him we would leave only if they came with us.

My Grandfather took hold of me and asked me to sing for him once more, then he forced my father to take us and leave. My grandmother gave my mother a bottle of milk for

Pawel. It was night and we were running through the dark and my mother tripped and dropped the bottle. It was the only thing we had from them …

Somehow the optimism that followed the Soviets' crossing of the old Polish border had faltered. During the very depth of winter there had been a spark of hope, but now as spring approached there seemed to be no end in sight. Frustration, intense irritation, humiliation, fury, resentment, all born of having to live under the most vile conditions, breathing the foul air, with nothing but memories to sustain them. 'How did I do it? I was like steel. I had become like steel,' Paulina reflected.

Chapter XV

'We scarcely noticed each other's appearance,' wrote Chiger, '… since we lived in twilight by the flickering carbide lanterns. We tried to maintain personal cleanliness, though it was difficult amidst the dirt and the mud.'

In fact the physical condition of the entire group, as well as their appearance, had deteriorated dramatically. They all had debilitating sores and rashes that periodically broke out over their bodies. Chiger for one recalled being covered in boils which tormented him and left him in despair. He claimed that they all seemed to disappear miraculously, though Klara recalled that they employed an 'old wives' remedy of grating raw potato and applying it to the boils – and this helped clear them up.

Other developments were more serious. Forced to spend most of their waking hours seated on the benches or on the floor, or, if they needed to move about, standing in permanently hunched-over positions, they suffered various physical deformations. Most of them developed curvature of the spine which made them appear to have a permanent stoop. Their legs swelled and their feet developed large sores. Their joints became stiff and fiercely painful. Their wrists and hands were also swollen, their skin had turned sallow and their eyes were beginning to fail under the constant flicker from the lamp. The general mental condition had also been stretched beyond reason and Chiger recalled their having to develop a sort of communal defence against the constant impulse simply to break down and weep uncontrollably.

In the crushing tedium of each day, a perfect copy of the day before, they had not noticed the gradual warming that had taken place in the air above. The snows had melted, the streams and rivers swelled and a new season had finally arrived. Along with this rejuvenation came the annual spring rains, which loosened the hard soil ready for the plough. The rains washed the city of winter debris, sweeping the streets and filling the sewers with fresh water.

Though Socha delivered a brief weather report whenever he was visiting, it had become difficult to relate these words to a real spring day. Memories of times past had become even more precious and the scent of warm air must have made the urge to step out into the sunshine almost unbearable. However, the first tangible proof that there had been a change in season was a rainstorm that broke one Sunday morning. It had started to rain before dawn and continued, hour after hour. Down in the catch basin, the incoming pipe was delivering a steady stream of water that splashed hard on to the floor, and then followed the shallow depression across to the exit pipe, the Seventy, on the other side. When Socha and his wife left their house for church it seemed as though the heavens were emptying all the water in the Ukraine on the town of Lvov alone. The drains had reached their capacity and the gutters had begun to overflow. Pavements were flooded, while manholes in the street were being lifted by the pressure of the water beneath. Socha could imagine precisely what was happening under the streets. The massive elliptical tunnels were filling with water, which meant the storm pipes had already filled to capacity. Socha was in despair as he watched the vast volume of water rushing down the streets and, as they entered the church, his thoughts were with the ten individuals trapped in the storm basin. For now he had come to realize the critical error he had made in leading them to that particular spot.

The sole function of a storm basin, sometimes called a holding reservoir or catch basin, was to regulate the flow of storm water during just such a cloud-burst. It was designed to collect a large body of water, retain it and check its flow into the sewers through a single exit pipe, so allowing a steady, constant flow to enter the system. A series of these underground basins were scattered throughout the system, usually situated midway down the slope of a hill to prevent the sewer pipes having to cope with a sudden explosion of water and bursting under the pressure. Its entire design and purpose, however, now threatened the lives of everyone hiding in it.

Beneath the cobbles on Bernadinski Square, the water coming through the inlet pipe in the basin had risen in pressure until it spewed forth against the opposite wall like a fire hose. The floor had flooded and the level risen above the aperture of the exit pipe. The water was entering more quickly than it was draining away. The basin was functioning perfectly – and the water level was rising.

Up and down the length of the room, tin cans, bottles, pots and buckets bobbed and floated in everybody's way. Chiger and some of the other men tried to find a way of blocking the inlet pipe with pots and pieces of clothing, but the terrific force simply blew anything straight out again. Margulies and Berestycki tried to retard the flow, by holding the blade of the shovel against the torrent, but again the pressure was overwhelming. Chiger and

Margulies, stripped down to their waists, tried pressing their bare backs against the pipe. By heaving themselves bodily against the torrent, they hoped to staunch the flow to allow sufficient water to escape again. They stood with their backs pressed hard against the wall but it had no effect at all. The water continued to pour in and the level continued to rise.

Throughout the service in the church, Socha listened to the relentless downpour on the roof. He could vividly imagine exactly what was occurring beneath the street – and there was nothing he could do about it.

If it had been a perfectly sealed unit, the air pressure might have been enough to stop the flow, but it was old and cracked, the walls pervious to both air and water, so the air escaped as quickly as the water rushed in. It had dawned upon everyone that they were all in mortal danger. As the water rose to halfway up the walls, Kristina became almost hysterical.

The waters had swallowed up the beds, the stoves and lanterns, everything had gone. All that remained was this precious and diminishing pocket of air. Kristina recalled: 'At the time I didn't understand what was happening, I only saw this huge amount of water coming through the pipe. People were panicking and crying ... I remember my father with his shirt off, standing against the pipe, trying to stop the water. It did no good ...' The only remaining precaution they could take was to make sure the exit pipe remained unclogged. Pots and pans were now at the bottom of the chamber and being dragged by the outward flow towards the Seventy. If that became blocked all hope would vanish. Paulina and her husband took hold of their children and tried to calm them, but they themselves were as close to sheer panic as everyone else. Kristina recalled: '... and this was the moment I thought that this is it, we are going to die.'

Socha imagined the terror of being trapped in the basin and he saw that the situation was hopeless. He lit a candle beneath the statue of the Virgin and buried himself in prayer.

Down in the basin, several members of the group had also resorted to prayer. Kristina remembered pleading with Berestycki: 'I remember I was crying and I was begging one of the men to pray. I begged him, Jacob, pray to God, pray to God!' The little girl was absolutely convinced that Berestycki was endowed with religious authority and that his prayers would be more effective. She believed completely, as only children can, that their existence was entirely in the hands of God, through the power of the holy man. It was for her the end of everything. Panic swept through her and she flailed about for an escape. ' "Tell God to stop the raining and the water will disappear." I was holding him and grabbing him – I felt this was the last resort.'

The water had risen up to their chins and they were trapped in a tiny pocket of air. For each and every member of the group there was a moment, an incident that characterized the entire ordeal and for Kristina this was the worst moment of crisis. Despite all that she had experienced before, it was during those few moments, as her mother pressed her hard up against the ceiling, that she truly confronted death.

The following morning, Socha and Wroblewski met up before entering the sewers. Neither of them were in any doubt about what had happened during the Sunday storm. It was one of their routine responsibilities to descend and check the main arteries for damage. What had haunted Socha all night was the prospect of finding the remains of his ten friends.

Wroblewski had agreed to enter the chamber first and report on the scene. But even before he had climbed into the Seventy, both men could tell from the sounds at the other end that they were both in for a surprise. Wroblewski and then Socha, doubtless struggling to control his emotions as he wriggled down the pipe, entered the chamber to see all ten standing before them. Chiger and Paulina described Socha's state as one of deep and profound shock. His conviction that they were all dead had been absolute. Now it was shattered and at first he found it hard to comprehend. All around everything was in ruin but salvageable. The floor was caked in mud which they had already begun to scrape away. Everyone and everything was still soaked – and would remain so for weeks. But everyone was alive, no one was even injured.

Kristina explained to Socha what had happened. She described her pleas to Jacob for prayers to stop the rain, and how, miraculously, the water had simply stopped pouring in through the pipe. That is exactly how all the accounts described it. Slowly, the flow of water coming in had diminished until it had weakened to a trickle, and the water had simply drained away. In the eyes of the seven-year-old child, it had been Berestycki's prayers. There could be no doubt.

'I was sure you were dead. I knew you were all dead,' Socha told Chiger. The effect on the sewer worker was profound. He told them that the following morning he had gone straight to church to light another candle; this time to give thanks. His interpretation had been as uncomplicated as Kristina's. It was, in his unshakeable opinion, absolute proof that his efforts were being observed and rewarded. It was divine confirmation that his 'mission' as he called it, was blessed. According to Chiger, his revelation upon entering their chamber '... filled him with renewed sense of purpose and commitment'. It apparently also had an evangelical effect on the recalcitrant Wroblewski, who was likewise charged with 'renewed persistence and endurance'.

There seemed to be a strengthening of the bond between Socha and Berestycki thereafter. These two deeply religious men had found a common link between their faiths that was to endure long afterwards.

Most of the group put their escape largely down to luck. But for some, the experience left an indelible mark. Their attempts to survive seemed to have been now crowned with a mystical quality, a sense that somehow it all had some purpose and meaning.

Another legacy of the flood was the psychological effect it had on a number of lives. Mrs Weinberg recounted many times that it had been the worst moment of the entire ordeal and that she had nightmares about it long afterwards. Kristina also admitted that she had never been so terrified. From that day forward, she found herself unconsciously listening to the sounds that drifted down from the street and the slightest hint of rain would send her almost hysterical with fear.

'Don't let it rain!' she would cry. 'Don't let it rain.'

Along with the warmer weather came further Soviet victories. In mid-March the Ukrainian armies to the south of Lvov had recaptured Odessa on the Black Sea and cut the Odessa-Lvov railway, while to the north, the Bug river, the new border between the Soviet Union and Poland, had been crossed at three places. By the beginning of April, Soviet armies to the south-west of Lvov had crossed the Romanian and Czechoslavakian borders. Due east of Lvov, along the line to Kiev, a great battle was being waged for the town of Tarnopol.

Chiger recorded that Socha gave them daily reports of the battle. On 15 April it was announced that Tarnopol had finally fallen to the Soviets. Their liberators were now less than 130 kilometres away. 'We were frantic with joy to hear the news,' wrote Chiger.

But the story of Tarnopol is a tragic one. Soon after the city had been liberated, a number of Jews who had been in hiding, emerged from their sanctuaries. Over the following weeks the Germans launched counter-attacks and the city fell once more to the invader. All those who had come out of hiding were rounded up and executed. A similar fate was meted out to the Polish families who had hidden those hapless souls during the last months of the occupation. Chiger wrote: 'When this news reached us I had such a nervous shock that I stopped believing in our eventual rescue. We were all affected badly by this bitter news.' By the end of the month the town was again in Russian hands, but it was now too late for celebrations.

During this time of deep depression, Berestycki delivered a ray of hope. According to the Berestycki account, 'It was at a time when we were so racked with pain we could barely move and we were all quite desperate.' Berestycki awoke one morning and told everyone he had a dream. 'It was a very important dream,' he said. 'Jacob's Dream', as it has come to be known, is one of the most precious incidents that has survived. To Berestycki himself it had a powerful spiritual, almost mystical quality. While others might not have shared his conviction, no one disputes what happened.

'I dreamt of a Rabbi last night,' Berestycki told them. 'An old Hasidic Rabbi I knew in Lodz. He had a small *schtiebul* [a room in a house used for prayer, as opposed to a synagogue] where my father and I used to go for prayer. He was very elderly and so I used to visit him and his wife each day, and bathe his wife's feet. Because I took such good care of them, the rabbi told me one day: "Jacob, you are blessed. In the hard times to come, you, your children and your children's children will escape the terror."

'Then, one day in 1938 he made a speech at the *schtiebul* during the High Holidays. It was about a year before the war broke out. The Rabbi said: "So, you are dressed up for the High Holidays. But if you knew what was coming, you would dress for a *schivah* [mourning], fast and pray for deliverance."

'The old Rabbi died that year – and, of course, he had been right. Well, I dreamt of him last night and in the dream he came to deliver a message. In my dream he said to me: "I have come to tell you that I have fulfilled my promise. You remember my blessing. You should know that you will be free on a particular day." He told me a day in the Hebrew calendar. I told him that I had lost track of the Hebrew calendar, but I knew what day it was in the secular calendar. So he told me the date in the secular calendar.'

Chiger wrote that Berestycki's words were 'astonishing' and that his dream 'was like an omen'. In his version, he said that Jacob asked if anyone had a birthday in July. Paulina said that her birthday was on the twenty-third. 'That is the day we will be free. Twenty-third of July.'

Chapter XVI

There are no accounts from any of the survivors of what thoughts they had on the night of 30 May – the anniversary of the start of their ordeal in the sewers. It appears that the collective memory had lost any grasp of time since the beginning of spring. Their physical and mental states, which had been deteriorating steadily, were made worse by the growing tension over when they would finally be liberated. The reports of Soviet successes became more piecemeal, especially during May when there was something of a hiatus on the Ukrainian front. The situation must have seemed desperately frustrating at times, as the Soviets had advanced past Lvov south of the Carpathian mountains and to the north, across the Bug river. It appeared that Lvov had been forgotten and news of the Western Allies landing on the French coast on 6 June would have been small comfort when so many other liberating armies seemed so close at hand.

In fact the Soviets did not begin their campaign to capture the city until well into June, though the Germans had been preparing their defences since April. Despite the deteriorating military situation, anti-Jewish policies were not altered at all. Leon Wells records in *The Death Brigade* that as late as May 1944 a Polish woman, having been betrayed by her daughter as one who had sheltered Jews, was hanged and the dozen or so people she had hidden shot.

In other respects, however, life in the city had deteriorated. People were subjected to sudden curfews, even greater shortages of food and ever more ruthless intolerance of civil disobedience. This meant Socha's deliveries became more irregular and this also increased anxieties amongst the ten. To compensate he brought reserve supplies of ersatz coffee, sugar, barley and lentils to them.

Then, towards the end of June, Socha brought them something quite astonishing. He arrived one morning to deliver the bread, crawled out of the Seventy with Wroblewski and was followed by someone else. A total stranger.

'This is Tola,' Socha announced.

The group stood staring in disbelief. They had not been given any warning that he would be bringing a stranger, but worse was to follow.

'Tola will by staying with you,' Socha explained.

Chiger was incredulous and demanded an explanation. According to Socha, Tola was a Russian soldier who'd been wounded and captured by the Germans. He'd been transported to Lvov to be hospitalized. Once recovered, he was due to be sent to Germany where he would join the ranks of hundreds of thousands of Russian 'slaves' labouring in German factories. However, while in the hospital, Tola had developed an attachment to a nurse named Michalina, who was Socha's sister-in-law. The romance had developed and Michalina had pleaded with Socha to save her Russian lover from deportation. Socha had been persuaded and agreed to hide young Tola until the city was liberated. Where better than in the storm basin beneath Berna-dinski Square? There was little any of them could do about Tola's presence. He was there for the duration.

For the first few days, Tola was content with having been given refuge. He kept to himself in the corner and avoided any unnecessary contact. He was terrified by the rats and never came to terms with them or the general level of filth that had to be endured. As for the ten, having recovered from the shock of his presence, they were pleased to see a new face. They relished describing how they had survived for more than a year beneath the streets. But their accounts of the hardships and distress began to play on Tola's spirits. They spoke with such resignation, mixed with intense frustration, that the poor Russian soon plunged into depression, 'paralysing his spirit'. Despite the occasional visits from Socha and messages from Michalina, he could not be stirred from his torpor.

This new aspect had a disquieting effect on the closely knit group. Tola's novelty value had worn off; his sullen presence soon became resented and they made certain he was under no illusions about that. The whole situation disintegrated as Tola became restless, pacing back and forth and declaring that he'd had enough.

'How can you sit here day after day? How can you survive with the two children? This is impossible. I cannot do it.' He told them he was going to escape.

When Socha returned the following day, Chiger and Margulies told him of this and described the fear this intruder had generated within the group.

'If he left he would surely be captured, interrogated and made to confess everything; how he had escaped, who gave him shelter, where he had been hiding and with whom. It would be a catastrophe.'

212

Socha agreed that if Tola were to escape he'd bring disaster on all of them. He brought them a pistol and left it in Chiger's charge to be used on Tola if necessary. It wasn't long before there was a confrontation. One day, while everyone was otherwise preoccupied, Tola made a grab for freedom and dived towards the Seventy. Margulies followed him with his own pistol drawn. Halfway down the pipe, Korsarz got hold of the Russian and pressed the muzzle of the pistol into his ribs.

'If you move any further down the pipe I'll kill you,' Margulies told him. He later recalled the Russian's desparation: 'Tola shouted that he needed to get out, to get some fresh air. I told him, "You can't escape. We won't let you. If you go out you'll get arrested."'

Tola protested, 'I won't tell them anything. You can trust me.'

'We can't trust anyone. Believe me, if you get caught, you'll talk. There's no such thing as silence. We can't let you go, you are with us now, till the end.'

Unconvinced, Tola tested Margulies's resolve and moved further down the pipe. Then he heard the hammer on the revolver being cocked … The two of them shuffled back down the pipe, to the chamber.

Tola was now effectively a prisoner. He was watched twenty-four hours a day, each of the men taking it in turns to hold the revolver. At times, when the Russian became restive and showed signs of panic, he was tied up and even force fed. There was by now a steely resolve that had suffused them all, a kind of defiant ruthlessness. Anyone who threatened their liberation now could expect no mercy.

Within a week, Tola had become resigned to his confinement and they no longer found it necessary to tie him up. Though his bouts of panic had ceased, he was never trusted sufficiently for them to be able to do away with the guard duty. However, in this new atmosphere, the Russian began to open up a little and to describe what he knew of the campaign against the Germans. With one remark he completely transformed the relationship and inspired them all with renewed hope.

'The Red Army is so close, it cannot help but occupy the city. We will take it, building by building, like we did in Tarnopol.' But in the telling of it, Tola betrayed a secret he had kept from everyone. He had not been captured, he was a deserter. Having been wounded he had left his unit and actually given himself up to the Germans. When the Russians finally took the city, as they surely would, his life would be worth less than if he was in German hands. If he was caught the best he might expect would be transportation to Siberia. More likely, it would be the firing squad. Again he plunged into a desperate depression, his miserable rantings filled everyone with loathing. Their only distraction was trying to imagine the events that were taking place above their heads.

Since the beginning of July, they had heard the Germans constructing their defences in the streets. Socha reported that great preparations were being carried out in the suburbs, that buildings were being commandeered and that reinforcements were arriving from the west. By the end of the first week of July they could hear from the sewers the sound of the Soviet artillery shelling the suburbs. The shelling gradually became louder, and was coupled with the sound of heavy machine-gun fire. At times they could hear the rhythmic crunch of boots across the cobbles and the barked orders of the officers. This rising level of activity and drama on the street above generated almost delirious excitement. When the explosions were at their most intense, the ground shook beneath them and they were instantly swept with waves of fright. The men, almost overcome with curiosity, decided to throw caution to the wind and sally forth to reconnoitre. They were about to do something which, just a few days before, they would have regarded as suicidal. Clearly, the adrenaline level was high, for they were barely conscious of the risk.

Led by Margulies, they shuffled down the Seventy and into the adjacent storm pipe which led up to the main square, where they collected water. Like most storm pipes, these were accessible from the street through manholes every hundred metres or so.

As they worked their way forward on their elbows, the leader was able to make out the increasingly bright rays of sunlight from above. Immediately above this was a narrow vertical shaft, in the walls of which were embedded a set of steel rungs. Cracks of daylight could be seen from around the edge of the manhole cover. Having climbed to the top of the ladder, they then had to heave up the steel cover, some three centimetres thick, and slip a stone in place to hold it open. Then each one took it in turns to climb the ladder and peer out into the street. They were in the very centre of Bernadinski Square. Though Chiger's sight was failing him, he strained to bring his little chink of the world into focus: 'I finally recognized the monastery and Bernadinski Church that was attached. I even saw a monk working in his vegetable patch.' That narrow glimpse was the first Chiger had seen of the outside world in over thirteen months. 'The fighting was so close I could hear individual shots and the rumble of tanks. We even heard the officers yelling orders about setting mines in the streets,' he recalled.

Each in his turn climbed the ladder and peered across the field of cobbles at the world that had been, for most of them, just a memory. Finally, Margulies led the way back: 'We replaced the cover and went back to the women and children, both frightened and heartened because the fighting was so near.'

That brief glimpse of the street and the activity upon it, though welcome, had the effect of restoring their watchfulness. They were all left with the impression that they were much closer to the surface than they had previously imagined. When they returned to the basin they encouraged everyone to speak only in whispers and move about with the least amount of noise. This new regime helped to heighten the tension.

Some time during early July (Chiger places it in June), they were all roused by the distant sound of digging. It seemed to be some way above their heads. They listened in silence to the regular chipping of pick axes and the soft scrape of shovels. The following day they heard the same sound again, perhaps a little louder. When Socha and Wroblewski turned up Chiger hushed everyone and asked the sewer workers to listen. There was no doubt, they were digging up the road right above their heads. Perhaps they had been discovered and the Germans were digging their way down to get them.

Socha dismissed this but left immediately with Wroblewski to investigate. Collecting Kowalow along the way, they marched down to Bernadinski Square. 'The Germans were digging tank traps and laying mines beneath the cobbles.' wrote Chiger. There was no doubt about it, they were digging right above the catch basin.

Down below, they were in no mood just to sit and await the outcome. The sound had become so loud that it seemed as though they might break through at any moment. Margulies had reached the same state of desperation as everyone else: 'I was certain, this was the moment. Now we are finished.'

In the meantime, the people around him seemed to have been

seized by an idea. They grabbed the shovel and whatever else they could find and began shovelling earth and the used carbide that had been dumped in a corner. They imagined that if they could fill up the section of the chamber immediately beneath where the Germans seemed to be digging, then nothing but further soil would be discovered. Once again panic was in the air. They hurled themselves at the task, perhaps knowing as they did so that there was little chance of shifting enough dirt in time. 'It would never have worked, but we were desperate,' Margulies recalled.

While this frantic activity took place below, Socha, Wroblewski and Kowalow had approached the officer in charge of the digging operation. Socha later told Chiger, 'Seeing the mines being laid, right above your heads, there was nothing for it. We began to argue with the Germans.'

Kowalow, summoning all the authority his overalls and boots could conjure, confronted the officer. 'There are gas pipes right beneath your feet! If you continue to dig you will rupture the pipes.'

Naturally, the Germans were angered by this interference. The buildings in the area were occupied by various military departments and had to be defended from the expected tanks and infantry. Yet here was a confrontation of two authorities. The might of the aristocratic Wehrmacht, setting about its business, confronted by the solid, matter-of-fact, plebeian self-confidence of the municipal sewer authority. According to Chiger the argument in the street attracted the attention of some of the officers and men in the adjacent houses, who came out to enquire about the hold up: 'They were furious that the defence precautions were being threatened by these men in overalls.' Soon the street was filled with men eager to impress their opinions on each other, while behind them, a squad of privates took the opportunity to lean on their shovels and have a smoke.

Kowalow and Socha spoke with impressive authority. If the Germans continued they faced ominous consequences.

'If you rupture the pipes, you will blow yourself, your men and all these buildings to pieces. The whole street will go up.'

There was no contest. Reluctantly, the order was given to cease the operation and the soldiers shouldered their shovels. Beneath the street, Chiger and the others felt fearfully helpless. Both Margulies and Chiger claimed this was the most dangerous moment, '… utterly beyond our control,' though they reflected upon it with widely differing philosophies.

For Margulies it was further testament of Socha's resourcefulness and persuasive authority: 'He was such a clever fellow. He did this and that's why they stopped digging. They left twelve mines all wired together.' For Chiger, it was the hand of Providence. 'No wonder Socha believed, now more than ever, that he had been chosen to save us.'

Throughout this incident and the days that followed, their thoughts and conversations were underscored by the incessant heavy thud of an artillery barrage. Klara recalled taking the children down the Seventy and going for walks through the larger pipes that criss-crossed the system: 'Every so often we would hear a loud bang and feel the vibrations through the ground.'

Then, somewhere in the midst of all this activity, around the third week of July, Socha failed to turn up with the bread. After the third day without sight of him or Wroblewski they became worried and were preoccupied with explanations for his absence. Perhaps the Germans had brought down a total curfew, the city was about to be razed to the ground prior to their retreat – just as they had done in Kiev. Meanwhile Tola '… began to rave like a madman and we feared he'd completely lose his mind through frantic despair,' wrote Chiger.

At this point others were becoming concerned about Chiger's own emotional state. He lashed out angrily at his wife and anyone else who questioned his authority. In his own account Chiger admits that he had reached a state of '... almost complete physical and nervous exhaustion', cut off from Socha he felt abandoned while great unknown events were being played out above.

During lulls in the fighting, Margulies stood with his ear pressed to the ceiling, listening for voices. He strained to hear the language that was spoken.

'Chiger, listen here. Listen to these voices. It's Russian!'

But there was something wrong. He could hear a mixture of tongues, perhaps Mongolian, perhaps some of the Muslim tongues from the central states of the Union.

'These are not the proper Russians, these are deserters,' Margulies said after some thought. Chiger became furious. 'I tell you the Russians are not there yet,' Margulies insisted.

The fourth day passed and still there was no sign of Socha. Chiger became obsessed with what had happened in Tarnopol. There developed a curious tension, something between growing excitement at the prospect of returning to the street, coupled with fear of the unknown.

It was perhaps an indication of his inner turmoil that at this point in Chiger's account his recollection seems to have failed him. He described an incident when 'Korsarz and Chaskiel went out for a few days', explaining that they took '... great care not to be seen by the Germans'. He went on: 'It was a sign that restrictions on the street were lessening. Our spirits were lifted by their reports and we began to believe that we would be saved.'

According to Margulies, however, no such 'excursions' took place. Neither he nor Chaskiel had made further trips to the street since October: 'We could barely get Chaskiel to take his turn to go for water any more. Besides, it was too dangerous.'

Indeed it was. The fifth day of their solitude, the 23 July, was Paulina's birthday. Like a surprise birthday present, they heard the familiar shuffle coming down the Seventy. Through the aperture emerged Wroblewski. He had come, partly to reassure them they had not been abandoned, but mostly to shelter from the fighting that was still raging above. The building he lived in had been hit and there was heavy fighting throughout his neighbourhood. The sewers seemed to be the only place to hide. Over the next few days, the sounds of fighting became more intermittent and eventually they ceased. It was over.

Some five days after his last visit, Socha finally arrived. He described what had been happening. The Germans, who had been all but surrounded, had decided not to fight for each and every building but instead retreated quietly one night leaving the city largely undamaged. There were pockets of resistance still, small garrisons that had been left behind to fight suicidal rearguard actions. Most of these were Ukrainian units, or White Russians who had fought in German uniforms. Nevertheless, the Red Army was now in occupation of Lvov.

Yet it was still not safe. In the buildings and alleyways, those small pockets of Ukrainian guerrilla units were holding out. Though they would eventually be flushed out, in the meantime they were conducting a campaign of murder against those who might bear witness to their co-operation with the Germans. Poles and Jews who had emerged from hiding were being picked off in the street. Socha claimed it would be a few days yet. Again, the spectre of Tarnopol rose before them. 'On the night of the twenty-sixth it was my turn to stand watch over Tola,' Chiger described in his account.

He was handed the revolver and took up his duty. While Tola was awake '… he had remained frantic and agitated by the sounds of Russian soldiers.' Despite the quiet from the street, Chiger still remained on edge. The following morning, Margulies rose from his bed and set off to fetch the day's water. One after the other, they all rose and began to tidy away the bedding material. Mrs Weinberg began to make coffee while someone else shifted the boards away to convert the beds into benches. Margulies returned within the hour with the water and began to shave. Chiger passed the revolver to Margulies.

'Your turn, Korsarz,' he said and crawled over to a bench to catch up on his sleep. The routine proceeded as it had done for fourteen months, until suddenly there was a loud banging on the grate above the inlet pipe.

'Korsarz! Chiger! Wake up!'

The voice, Socha's, came from out in the street.

'You're coming out.'

Margulies put down his razor and shuffled over to the pipe.

'What?'

'You can come out. Go to the nearest manhole, I'll be waiting there.'

Margulies didn't need any further encouragement. He told them he would be back soon and then almost dived into the Seventy and began elbowing his way towards the other end.

Chiger, sound asleep, hadn't heard a word. The others were at first frozen with disbelief. Margulies had gone so quickly they hardly had time to absorb what was happening.

'We're going out?' Klara enquired, disbelievingly.

Margulies found his way down a storm pipe towards a brilliant beam of light that flooded the pipe from above. Though Socha's voice echoed down through the sunlight, Margulies could see nothing in the glare. Blindly, he climbed the rungs up the wall of the shaft and, with Socha's steadying hand, stumbled into the street.

For the first time, Socha could see the man in the daylight and was shocked at the deep yellow pallor of his skin. He was jaundiced. Margulies's eyes stung with the intensity of the glare. Later he remembered nothing of the scene, except the colour. Everything seemed bathed in blood. Socha took him and led him into the gloomy hall of an apartment block. His eyes began to re-focus, though everything still seemed bathed in a curious blood-red colour.

Margulies followed Socha to a rear door that led into the courtyard. In the ground there were two manholes, the tunnels from which led back into the storm pipes.

As Socha heaved against the covers, the caretaker came out to see what was happening.

'What is this. Jesus and Mary! Where have you come from?'

'Shhhh!' whispered Margulies.

She stood there, stunned by this apparition in her courtyard, but she was clearly not going to get any explanation. Socha explained to Margulies what he must do. Follow the pipe that led from the manhole, it would lead him to the storm pipe and then to the chamber. 'Lead them out to here. It's better than the street because they'll have more shelter.'

Margulies might have assumed he meant from the daylight, but in fact Socha was concerned about the sporadic shooting that still echoed up and down the narrow streets. Taking another look at the world, Margulies slipped down the manhole into a small brick-lined chamber, no more than thirty centimetres beneath the floor of the courtyard. He was amongst the foundations of the building. Two pipes led away from him, one that led under the hall, towards the street, and another, at right-angles under the building, towards the Bernadinski Church. That was the direction Socha had indicated. The pipe, a Forty, continued for about fifteen metres then suddenly dipped and ran downhill for a couple of metres, before levelling out and connecting with a storm pipe. The pipe was so narrow and the going so difficult that he could feel the skin being scraped from his elbows and knees. He returned to the catch basin to find everyone assembled before him.

'It's true. We're all coming out!' Paulina recalled Margulies's words: 'Pepa and the children first, then the rest of the women. Halina, Klara, Mrs Weinberg. Then Tola, Chaskiel, Berestycki and the last one, the captain of the ship, Chiger.'

They took nothing with them. They simply dropped what they had in their hands and moved to the entrance of the Seventy. Chiger completed scribbling something on a scrap of newspaper, folded it up tightly and wedged it into a crack in the chamber wall. The kerosine stove was turned off, the light of the carbide lamp doused. One by one, they crawled down the Seventy, following Korsarz's lead. They squeezed into the Forty and followed it, with great difficulty, up the incline towards a growing blaze of light. With every bend in the pipe, the light would disappear and then appear again. Eventually they were all crouched amongst the red brick walls of the building's foundations, penetrated by a sharp and painful glare from above. Margulies guided each one towards the manhole, where Socha stood ready to haul them out.

In the courtyard a small crowd had gathered around the opening, and above their heads, staring from the balconies and doorways of the apartments, further spectators craned to catch a view. Russian soldiers too had arrived to investigate the commotion. To the collective sounds of a mixture of horror and amazement, Socha reached down into the hole and pulled out a dark-coloured, filthy creature. An emaciated, foul-smelling, crooked hag; her back hunched over, her hands covering her face from the glare. Behind her, another: smaller, a child, a girl. Again the back doubled over. Blind. Clothes dark with grime. Then another child: smaller still, a boy, with a look of utter terror on his face.

One by one these creatures of the underworld clambered out into the sunlight, blind and helplessly weak. Tears streaked their faces. 'Everything around me was red. Red-orange. The faces were red, the buildings were red, the sky was red,' recalled Kristina. 'I saw no colour at all,' remembered Klara. 'After the blindness had passed, I saw everything in black and white. And I was ashamed. I was embarrassed, in front of all those people. I had just that one coat for the whole fourteen months, I looked so shabby. I was embarrassed.'

When Berestycki emerged he was so lame he had to be helped to one side and laid down on the concrete floor. They were all without shoes and their feet were covered in bleeding sores. Orenbach weighed less than thirty-eight kilos when he emerged. The tall, tragic beauty he clung to, a few kilos more.

Klara, overwhelmed with joy, threw herself at Paulina and kissed her gratefully. 'Thank you for saving me. Without you …'

Pawel, when finally he could bear to look in the light, saw this crazy red-coloured world filled with space, air, and faces. He threw himself into his mother's arms and buried himself in her warmth. 'I want to go back. I want to go back, I am afraid,' he cried.

In tears and choking anguish, he searched for the familiar. Above their heads was an oddly shaped polygon of bright red sky, and everywhere staring faces, stunned, disbelieving, silently shaking their heads. And there, in the midst of all the chaos, Socha stood proudly, staring his fellow countrymen in the eye.

'This is my work. All my work. These are my Jews.'

Chapter XVII

O nce the news had spread, people came running down to Bernadinski Square and crowded into the narrow hall to try and catch a glimpse of the creatures from the sewers. The little courtyard became packed with people straining to hear the story. Standing in their midst, Leopold Socha patiently told and retold his account for those who would listen. A pair of Russian soldiers who had been sitting on the lawn in front of the Bernadinski Church barged through the throng to investigate and the story was told once more. They had entered the sewers on the 1 June 1943, and emerged on 28 July 1944. It had been fourteen months.

Meanwhile, the ten sat on the concrete or staggered about, shielding their eyes from the light. Tola had escaped into the crowd almost as soon as his eyes could cope with the light. (Eventually he returned to the army but died during the campaign in Germany.) The concierge became infected with the miracle that had taken place beneath her feet and declared before the audience that she had often been puzzled by the smell of fried onions.

'Mrs Weinberg's soup!' Socha confirmed.

'I always thought it was from food that had been thrown down the drains. I never thought anyone was actually cooking in the sewers.' This was greeted with ripples of laughter and the incredulous shaking of heads. They had become, for the time being, specimens to be pointed to and gazed at. 'We emerged like cavemen. We had nothing. Our clothes nothing more than rags and our appearance frightened people,' wrote Chiger.

For many of those creatures of the underworld, the return to the street was just too much and they became emotional. Uncontrollable tears mingled with cries of relief as they hid their faces from the piercing stare of the unbelievers. They had emerged from one ordeal to be thrown into another. Socha and Margulies both realized that everyone needed to find shelter from the curious. Socha had learnt that the building had been occupied by the Germans, but was now vacated. The two of them climbed the stairs to the first floor to investigate. They found the rooms empty but locked. They also found one solitary German soldier who had been left behind by his compatriots. He was a noncombatant, a war artist in fact, whose job it had been to record the great Russian front. The concierge knew about him.

'He's harmless,' she told them. Harmless and terrified at the sight of Korsarz as it happened. Ignoring the hapless German, Margulies broke the lock on the first room and went inside. There were three adjoining rooms and a furnished kitchen. It would be ideal. However, as they moved back into the corridor they were confronted by a Russian officer with a large ring of keys.

'What are you doing here? These rooms have been confiscated,' said the Russian.

'Yes! By us!' replied Margulies.

The Russian brandished his keys, but when he tried two or three in the lock, he could not open it.

'You have keys to nothing!' exclaimed Margulies. 'These are all our rooms – the lot!'

Socha returned to the courtyard and began shepherding his flock towards the stairs. 'How long do you think you will sit here? You will be a lady again, just as you were before,' he told Paulina. 'See, you already have a room ...'

'My wife and I and the children occupied one room, the "Pirate" and Jacob the second room, Halina and Klara the third, and Chaskiel and Mrs Weinberg the fourth. Stefak had already begun collecting furniture – chairs, tables, beds and bedding,' recalled Chiger. Paulina took Kristina and Pawel up to the window and opened it, though their eyes were still stinging from the blood-red light.

'Breathe the air,' she said. 'Breathe deeply the fresh air.'

As they stood there, Paulina looked down upon the street and the small piece of grass opposite, where a crowd had gathered. There, standing in the street, was an old friend. Chiger looked over his wife's shoulder and agreed: 'They were old friends of ours from the athletic club.' It must have seemed a hundred years ago.

'Mischa! Mischa!' Paulina called from the window. Her friend looked up and then tugged at her husband's sleeve. They both stared up at the vision at the window.

'Pepa? Chiger? Is it you?'

The couple pushed their way through the crowd and up the stairs. When they got to the room they stared at the frail shapes silhouetted at the window.

'The children?'

'Here. Alive. We are all here.'

'But Chiger?' they said. 'We always knew you would make it. You were too clever ...'

Chiger recalled the great kindness offered them:

They had with them a bottle of vodka and some kielbasa which they shared with us. We celebrated and rejoiced in seeing each other again. As we drank they told us that they had heard that Pepa and the children had been dragged away by the SS … Later they returned with more food. Over the next few days we had many visitors, most of them strangers. One woman brought honey, another brought bread …

All the people were amazed. 'I heard that you survived with two children …' they would say. 'I heard the story of the children from the sewers …'

The process of healing was a slow one. For some, there would never be a full recovery. 'Mrs Weinberg was never the same. She was not a well person from the day we left the sewer. Very highly strung and emotional, but would sit on her own in complete silence. I don't remember ever having a conversation with her,' recalled Klara.

Genia and Chaskiel moved out of the apartment block to another part of the city. Though they remained in touch with the group, they rarely saw them again.

The rest of the 'family' stayed together for some time while they found their strength and the courage to walk the streets again. But before they could begin to think of the future, Chiger's group had to re-learn the basics. They got used to sleeping in beds again and moving about in a room where the ceiling was nearly three metres from the floor. After four years of isolation they had to get used to walking along open streets and through a community no longer encouraged to treat them like base animals. The most dramatic change in their lives was the simple fact that the night lasted only until dawn, and that the day did not end with the dousing of a lamp, but with a bright golden sunset. Some old habits, however, they were obliged to keep up. Like lentil and potato soup.

As the rooms were being furnished, Chiger and Socha had returned to the sewers to retrieve everything that might be of use; stoves, jugs, pots and pans. Chiger wrote: 'We left behind only those things which were of no use, like rags and torn newspapers which had served as pillows. Socha brought his wife and child to meet them. Wanda, of course, had shared in helping to save our lives.'

In the months that followed, they had other visitors too. Leon Wells had survived the Janowska camp and, while walking the streets of Lvov, ran into his friend Berestycki:

> We had worked for a while in the same shop, he as a mechanic and I as an assistant to a plumber. He was on crutches; his feet were as abraded as mine had been. We embraced each other and he invited me to his apartment nearby. I went with him. Berestycki cooked a meal for me at his apartment. When he gave me the steaming plate of cereal, it smelled awful. He was still using the leftover supplies from the sewer, which had spoiled and had also been penetrated by the terrible sewer odour.

Over this meal Wells was introduced to the others and told the story of their escape to the sewers. Berestycki also offered Wells somewhere to stay. He claimed that there were plenty of abandoned apartments in the floors above, which had been sealed off

229

by the Russian police. 'Without much hesitation we decided then and there that we would break the seal. After all, what could they do to us?' recalled Margulies.

During the following year they found work and some stability to their lives. Halina found a job in the office of the railway department and in turn helped the nineteen-year-old Leon Wells find work there. Everyone found some way of earning money. Chiger got a job with the district sports authority which, though unpaid, provided him with tickets he could exchange for food. Paulina baked potato pancakes and sold them on the street. They made a fortuitous discovery of a large barrel of German army boot-polish, which they scooped into smaller tins and Kristina and Pawel sold on the street for a few kopeks. Margulies thrived doing what he was best at.

Within two months they were back on their feet, putting their lives back together. Leon Wells moved to another apartment and Berestycki moved in with him. 'Berestycki was a very easy going fellow,' wrote Wells. 'He worked, if one could call it that, at the tourist office and … by fixing locks and doing some plumbing. He would never do more than he needed to for his daily expenses.' According to Wells's account, Berestycki had soon rediscovered his love for life. He was determined to go to a dance every night and being short and dark he was naturally attracted to tall blondes. And he had a system: 'To go dancing, one had to buy at least one beer, which cost five rubles. Berestycki would buy one beer, and then take the glass home and sell it the following day on the black market for five rubles. He would then be all set for the next evening.'[17]

In September, Paulina queued up at the public school to enrol her daughter for first grade. Paulina had to answer a long series of questions about the child, and when she answered the question concerning religion, there was a long pause while the clerk sought advice from the superintendent.

'Not possible. How could this be? Hadn't they all been annihilated?'

* * *

Throughout that first year they scratched a living while waiting for their repatriation. Lvov was, of course, no longer part of Poland, but of the newly extended Republic of the Ukraine – part of the Soviet empire. Under the new regime, it quickly became obvious that there was no hope of retrieving any of their property. The brief period of Sovietization that had begun in 1940 was taken up again with a vengeance as soon as the machinery of government was in place. Under the circumstances, most Poles sought permission to travel across the new border, to where they imagined they would find a post-war society more to their liking. The Soviets were obliged to let them go.

The first to leave was Berestycki. With him on the same train to Lodz were Chaskiel Orenbach and Mrs Weinberg, now more tragic than ever. The two of them had worked hard to save as much money as they could, to try and 'buy back' Genia's last surviving child. She had given the baby girl to Ukrainians for safe keeping, before entering the ghetto. They had made contact with the foster parents, but at the rendezvous under a railway bridge where they had agreed to hand over the money for the child, they had been cheated. They were glad to see the last of Lvov.

When Berestycki returned to Lodz he was appalled. The little chap had somehow imagined that what had happened in Lvov was some terrible perversion, exclusive to that city. When he discovered the same and worse had been visited throughout Poland – and upon all the occupied countries – he could barely comprehend it. Jacob met a young friend from his old neighbourhood, a survivor from Auschwitz, and they were married.

By the new year, those still in Lvov began noticing the more unhealthy aspects of the Soviet system. People's pasts were being investigated for evidence of any pre-war anti-Soviet activity. Many were being tried and imprisoned. Socha, a most patriotic Pole, suddenly informed the Chigers that he was taking his wife and child to Przemysl, just inside the Polish border. The Chigers too, began to suspect they were under investigation, for any Jew who had survived the German occupation had become an object of suspicion. In February, they slipped quietly across the border and went to live with Socha and his family. And just in time: 'Korsarz later told us that a few hours after we left Lvov the KGB had come to arrest us. They sealed off our apartment and searched the railway cars,' wrote Chiger.

After three weeks the Chigers left the Sochas in Przemysl and moved to Krakow. In April 1945, just before the end of the war in Europe, Halina also left for Poland where she made plans to emigrate to the United States of America. The last to cross over were the Margulies family. Mundek and Klara had been married and already had a son. They settled in the town of Gliwice and were joined by Socha and his family. Within a matter of a few months the survivors had been scattered across Poland, though they kept in touch. Letters and money were passed back and forth and through this network the various families were able to find some small way of expressing their gratitude to Socha. They all contributed to the purchase for Socha of a small bar in Gliwice. It was something he had always wanted, his own little place, his own small business. 'It made him very proud,' recalled Paulina.

Though they were scattered to the four winds and all making their separate plans to emigrate to the west, they were only too soon reunited. On 12 May 1946, Socha and his daughter Stepya were out together riding their bicycles. As they peddled down a steep hill, Socha saw a Russian army truck careering madly across the road in Stepya's path. He desperately peddled ahead, overtook his daughter and knocked her safely out of the path of the truck. Within the same instant, Socha had collided with the juggernaut and under the mangled bicycle frame, Socha's broken body lay lifeless. 'He had fallen over a drain in the street, and his blood flowed freely into the sewer,' wrote Chiger.

The Chigers received the telegram the following day and took the next train. Within the week, they were all together again, to march behind Socha's widow and child to the funeral. There were no words to describe their sadness as they gathered at Socha's house afterwards. Chiger, his family and friends stood with Catholics and thought themselves united in grief. Then someone was heard to say from the back of the room, 'This is God's retribution. This is what comes of helping the Jews.'

Notes

1 Drawn from *The Death Brigade*, by Leon Wells and interviews with Mundek Margulies.

2 Drawn from David Lee Preston, 'A Bird in The Wind', *Enquirer* magazine; (8 May 1983).

3 Virtually all material concerning Jacob Berestycki comes from a series of interviews made with his son, Prof Henri Berestycki and widow, Mrs Gutche Berestycki, in Paris during October 1989.

4 Letter from Jan Felix, 16 August 1989. He had survived the liquidation by escaping to the forests. His fair hair and blue eyes disguised his origins and enabled him to move back to the city, where he scavenged off the streets. He was about 15 years old when Lvov was liberated.

5 Leon Wells, *op cit.*, p. 129.

6 Reuben Ainsztein, *Jewish Resistance in Nazi-occupied Eastern Europe*, (London, ELEK, 1974) pp. 444–5.

7 Joachim Schoenfeld, *Holocaust Memoirs* (KTAV, 1985), p. 119.

8 Drawn from Leon Wells, *op. cit.*, p. 130.

9 These figures have been calculated with the help of

Dr Bullen at the Imperial War Museum, London; and with reference to Richard Lucas, *The Forgotten Holocaust* (University Press of Kentucky, 1986).

10 Stefan Szende, *The Promise Hitler Kept*, (London, Gollancz, 1945), p. 271.

11 Leon Wells, *op. cit.*, p. 208.

12 Sigmund Heimer, BBC interview, August 1988. He escaped from the Janowska camp during an uprising in November 1944, and joined the partisans.

13 Leon Wells, *op. cit.*, p. 206.

14 The Continental school of higher education, preparing pupils for university.

15 Drawn from David Lee Preston, *op. cit.*

16 *Krushchev Remembers*, trans. and ed. Strobe Talbott, p. 139.

17 Leon Wells, *op. cit.*, pp. 267–71.

Bibliography

Academy of Sciences of the Ukraine SSR, Institute of State and Law, *Nazi Crimes in the Ukraine 1941–1944* (Kiev, Naukova Dumka, 1987).

Reuben Ainsztein, *Jewish Resistance in Nazi-occupied Eastern Europe* (London, ELEK, 1974).

Mark Arnold-Forster, *The World at War* (London, Collins, 1973).

P. E. Baker, J. M. Eltenton, N. Hall and H. Stannard, *Chronology of the Second World War* (London, Royal Institute of International Affairs, 1947).

Nicholas Bethell, *The War Hitler Won, September 1939* (London, Penguin, 1972).

Yuri Boshyk (ed.), *Ukraine During World War II: History and Aftermath* (Canadian Institute of Ukrainian Studies, University of Alberta, Edmonton, 1986).

Norman Davies, *Heart of Europe, a Short History of Poland* (OUP, 1986).

Encyclopaedia Judaica, vol 11 (New York, Macmillan, 1972).

Martin Gilbert, *The Holocaust, the Jewish Tragedy* (London, Collins, 1986).

Martin Gilbert, *The Holocaust, Maps and Photographs* (Board of

Deputies of British Jews, 1978).

Maria Hochberg-Marianska, *Children Accuse* (Jerusalem Jewish Historical Commission, 1947).

Shmuel Krakowski, *The War of the Doomed: Jewish Armed Resistance in Poland, 1942–1944* (London, Holmes and Meier, 1984).

Krushchev Remembers, trans. and ed. by Strobe Talbott (London, Deutsch, 1971).

James Lucas, *War on the Eastern Front 1941–1945* (London, Jane's, 1979).

Richard C. Lucas, *The Forgotten Holocaust, the Poles Under German Occupation 1939–1944* (The University Press of Kentucky, 1986).

Michael R. Marrus, *The Holocaust in History* (London, Weidenfeld and Nicolson, 1987).

Murray S. Miron and Arnold P. Goldstein, *Hostage* (London, Pergamon, 1979).

Vladimir Molchanov, *The Killers' Whereabouts Are Known* (Moscow Novostí Press, 1986).

E. L. Quarantelli (ed.), *Disasters: theory and research* (New York, Sage, 1978).

Joachim Schoenfeld, *Holocaust Memoirs, Jews in the Lwow Ghetto, the Janowski Concentration Camp and as Deportees in Siberia* (Hoboken, KTAV, 1985).

Stefan Szende, *The Promise Hitler Kept* (London, Gollancz, 1945).

Leon Weliczker Wells, *The Death Brigade* (London, Macmillan, 1963).

Simon Willenberg, *Surviving Treblinka* (London, Basil Blackwell, 1989).

A NOTE ON THE AUTHOR

Robert Marshall divided his career between writing books and plays. He also produced arts and history programming initially for the BBC and, later, live recordings of great theatre productions for cinema release, with more than 100 credits to his name.

His writing career began with a series of radio plays, and a Play for Today 'Before Water Lilies' for the BBC in the 1970s. During the 1980s and 90s he scripted and directed over thirty programmes for the BBC, from documentaries to dramas including *All the King's Men* (1988) which was optioned by Stanley Kubrick, *In the Sewers of Lvov* (1990) which was made into the feature film *In Darkness*, and *Storm From the East* (BBC 1994) which was top of the Times non-fiction best-selling list for over two months. He became Executive Producer for The Globe on Screen, at Shakespeare's Globe Theatre.